CRAIG BROWN

Craig Brown writes regular columns for *The Times*, *The Sunday Times*, the *Independent on Sunday* and *Private Eye*. He lives with his wife Frances and their children Tallulah and Silas in Essex. A book of his selected journalism, 'Greatest Hits', will be published by Century in Autumn, 1993.

WALLACE ARNOLD

Wallace Arnold is widely recognised as our foremost social and political commentator. A legendary broadcaster, renowned as much for his off-the-cuff humour as for his wide-ranging knowledge of the arts and society, he was a member of the original panel not only of *Stop the Week* and *Any Questions?* but also of *Gardener's Question Time* and *My Music*.

In 1990, his appearance with Anthony Clare *In the Psychiatrist's Chair* involved no fewer than eleven complete breakdowns, easily establishing a record for that popular series. A veteran of Royal broadcasts, he received the CBE from The Queen in 1983, and in 1986 had the great honour to be invited to accompany Their Royal Highnesses The Duke and Duchess of York on their honeymoon.

Many of the pieces first appeared in *the Independent on Sunday, The Spectator* ~~and the Literary~~ *Review*. The Reminisc~~ences were originally~~ broadcast on Radio ~~4.~~

D1464921

WELCOME TO MY WORLDS!

The Dread Decades of
WALLACE ARNOLD

edited by Craig Brown

ARROW

Arrow Books Limited
20 Vauxhall Bridge Road, London SW1V 2SA

An imprint of Random House UK Ltd

London Melbourne Sydney Auckland Johannesburg
and agencies throughout the world

First published in 1993 by Arrow

Phototypeset by Intype, London

Printed and bound in Great Britain by
Cox & Wyman Ltd, Reading, Berks

ISBN 0 09 925931 1

For Alistair, Eva, Alexander and Charlotte

Contents

Acknowledgements

Once again, my thanks are due to HRH Queen Elizabeth the Queen Mother, that inveterate 'radio ham', for supplying me with transcripts of numerous private telephone conversations recorded from the telephone booth at Balmoral. I must also thank Baroness Thatcher and all at the headquarters of the Thatcher Foundation for the research grant that enabled me to complete the remaining chapters of this book in the comparative comfort of a suite at Claridge's Hotel, Mayfair.

Quite apart from his munificence in throwing open the doors of his hot and cold beverage cabinet to further the cause of my refreshment(!), Mr John Birt most generously 'shelved' over ninety hours of the more heavygoing wireless documentaries in order to finance my own award-winning retrospective. I am only thankful that his gamble paid off, and that, after so many recent embarrassments, the BBC is now firmly back on its feet.

I have decided to allow all four episodes of my wireless retrospectives to be published here for the first time after repeated requests from listeners the length and breadth of the country. Armed with these transcripts, families will now be able to re-create those memorable broadcasts within the comfort of their own sitting rooms. Who knows? Such a cheery recreation might stimulate a plucky member of today's younger gener-

ation to set his cap at becoming the Wallace Arnold of
the future!

W. A.
Antibes Cap Ferrat
Sandringham Monte Carlo
Auchtermuchty Mayfair
September 1992

Among the Thugs

GRANTA: DELICIOUSLY BLEAK

As the marketing director of that fine and 'gritty'(!) paperback magazine *Granta*, I am delighted that the first book by our esteemed Editor, Mr Bill Buford, has drawn so many sterling reviews in all parts of our national press from some of his most loyal contributors.

It was nye on twelve years ago that I handpicked Bill for the post of Editor. For some time, I informed him, I had sensed an untapped market for a glossy paperback magazine which the general reader would feel happy to leave lying on his or her bookshelf.

The Contents page was, our market research told us, by far the most important, being the only page read by over 53% of purchasers. After thorough investigation, we discovered that our thoroughly 1980s targeted readership was after a fashionable young name in bold type beside a suitably stark, 'gritty'(!) title. To this end, I drafted a dummy contents page for our first issue, 'Dirty Fingernails'. I have it with me now:

Martin Amis In the Launderette

Don McCullin Old Woman Eating Sand on Wolverhampton Beach

Raymond Carver Why the John Won't Flush

Richard Ford No Ketchup, No Relish Tray, No Burger, Nothing

Redmond O'Hanlon On Bruce Chatwin

Bruce Chatwin On James Fenton

James Fenton On Redmond O'Hanlon

David Hare Taking Brecht to Nicaragua

Hanif Kureishi Milton Keynes

Don McCullin Cross-Eyed Man With Empty Shopping Bag

Alas, Bill's first reaction was somewhat iffy. Was it not a little too . . . bleak? he asked.

'My dear boy,' I replied, taking a deep puff on my trusty pipe, 'The bleaker the better! Our marketing men assure me that the poor old bookbuyer is simply *crying out* for a spot of bleakness. First, he buys his black polo-neck from Next, then his matt black cafetière from Conran, and then – bob's your proverbial uncle – he nips out to buy his pile of Grantas for his matt black bookshelf. Hey presto: business booms!'

Within a few weeks, all the pieces had been commissioned and knocked off, and within a couple of months 'Issue 1: Dirty Fingernails' was on the bookstands, selling like hot-cakes. This was followed by 'Issue 2: More Dirty Fingernails', and then by 'Issue 3: More Dirty Fingernails Again'. We had, it was now safe to say, tapped a rich vein: the young Briton, having left his public school and university (or polytechnic!) was only too keen to be seen with an easy-to-handle glossy status-symbol, replete with vivid pen-portraits of nervous breakdowns in Notting Hill laundromats and elegant descriptions of working-class murders in out-of-the-way places.

At around this time, with sales blossoming, Bill began to get twitchy. Perhaps, he suggested, the readers were getting bored with the delightfully-named 'Dirty Realism'. Perhaps they would prefer all the same writers, but writing about something a little, well ... different?

Frankly, I slapped him down pretty sharpish: 'Such as what, may one ask?'

From out of his matt black briefcase, Bill brought forth a dummy contents page for 'Issue 4: Introducing Clean Realism'. I stared at his list in growing dismay:

Martin Amis The Magic of Julie Andrews

Don McCullin The Sun Has Got His Hat On

Raymond Carver It's a Funny Old World It Really Is

Richard Ford Welcome to the Fabulous World of Fondue

Frankly, I could read no further. Our customers, I retorted, would not tolerate such a revolution. They expected consistency from a market leader, and, in the case of Granta, this meant a rich diet of unfortunate occurences in faraway countries written in straightforward prose. Bill ummed and erred for a time, but eventually he saw reason. 'Okay,' he sighed (he is – needless to say! – an American), 'I'll send Hanif to Guatemala again,' and with that he picked up the phone.

Ten years on, the 'Dirty Realism' format still thrives, and though I am, as you might imagine, more of an *Illustrated London News* man myself, the readers, some of them now grown-up and with children of their own, still can't get enough. Bill, too, has finally seen sense. He had wanted his first book to be called *Among the Toffs*, a witty guidebook to the English social season. Happily, I persuaded him to retitle it *Among the Thugs*, and I am delighted to say that his close circle of reviewers has made sure that it is now available from all good second-hand book shops everywhere.

Backstage with Lord Ridley

A BRACE OF TRIBUTES TO AN OLD QUAFFING PARTNER

I

I have the very greatest affection for my old friend and quaffing partner Nicholas Ridley, but I wonder if he ever really found his niche in life?

I first met him backstage at The Royal Court theatre in Sloane Square in May or June, 1956. A young actor, fresh from RADA, he had been cast in the role of Jimmy Porter in John Osborne's splendidly caustic (if a mite working-class!) drama set at the end of the Central Line, originally titled *Look Back in Ongar*, playing opposite Mary Ure and the young Alan Bates.

'A tall thin young man wearing a very worn tweed jacket,' was the way Johnnie Osborne had described him in the introductory notes, 'Clouds of smoke fill the room from the cigarettes he is smoking ... restless, importunate, full of pride, a combination which alienates the sensitive and insensitive alike. Blistering honesty, or apparent honesty, like his, makes few friends'.

This was the young Nick to a T, and in rehearsal his fellow actors found it hard to fathom whether he was reciting his lines ('Shut up will you or I'll pull your ears off') or merely engaged in his workaday banter. Even at that early stage, he was very strict concerning cigarettes: if the script required him to be smoking, and a sudden break in rehearsals ensued, he would place one of his own cigarettes in his mouth alongside the cigarette already there. I well recall once coming across him with three cigarettes in his mouth – his own, his character's, and a third on loan from a stage-hand who had been called away to shift some heavy scenery.

Alas, after a promising start, Nick's acting career never really prospered. He was, I think, hopelessly miscast in the role of Buttons opposite Helen Shapiro's Cinderella in the pantomime of the same name at the Palladium in '59. Indeed, his portrayal of Buttons so terrified many of the younger members of the audience that during one matinee performance a group of distraught parents interrupted his spirited rendition of 'I'm a Jolly Little Fellow called Buttons, And I Puff-Puff-Puff All Day' with the demand that the safety curtain be lowered forthwith.

He was next to surface in 1967, in the first edition of *Penguin Modern Poets 10* – *The Mersey Sound*, an anthology of the four most notable Liverpool Poets of the time. His work differed from the others – Henri, Patten, McGough – in that his was the only truly *aristocratic* Liverpudlian voice among them. Though he had little knowledge of Liverpool ('bloody awful dump from all accounts') his great-grandfather had acquired extensive land there and, his lawyers argued to Penguin Books, in poetry as in property, possession is nine-tenths of the law. Alas, critics noted that his verse lacked some of the acute sensitivity to everyday life displayed by his fellow Liverpool Poets ('Ferry across the Mersey' began one poem, 'Bloody chilly, put on Jersey') and his selection was dropped from all subsequent editions.

In the early seventies, Nick appeared in the famous Hockney portrait *Mr and Mr Ossie Clark with their cat and Mr Ridley*, a piece very much of its time, in which that quintessentially fashionable couple lounge elegantly on a sofa while, towards the right hand side, Mr Ridley could be observed puffing away on a cigarette, wrestling with the accounts. Later, on impulse, Hockney was to alter the portrait, air-brushing out the figure of Ridley, replacing it with an attractive Ming dynasty wall-vase in aquamarine with an exotic inlay of deepest crimson.

After an unhappy few months playing on glockenspiel with the experimental German rock group Kraftwerk, Nick finally entered Parliament as a Conservative, his hat now set firmly against a Federal Europe. I fancy he must have derived some small satisfaction from his parliamentary career, and his name will be remembered for as long as his much under-rated Community Charge holds sway upon these shores, but at what cost, one wonders, to his inner self?

II

I wonder if anyone read my old friend and quaffing partner Nick Ridley's splendid article on the need for good manners gracing the pages of *The Times* last week? He began it in a lively, provocative fashion with the sentence, 'I happen to think that "good manners" are very important'. Two thousand words later, he ended with a typically elegant flourish: 'I do think we should all strive to have good manners'. In between, he put forward a closely-argued case for tact, courtesy and consideration – if any of these words still have a scintilla of meaning to the general reader in the latter half of the 20th Century (dread era!).

Nick – now Lord! – Ridley and I go back yonks, long before he rose to the giddy heights of Mrs Thatcher's Cabinet. Following an early hiccup in front of the Sutton and Cheam constituency selection committee – asked by the Chairman where he stood on the vexed question of an Incomes Policy he replied, 'What's it to you, fatface?' – Nick eventually found a safe seat in Cirencester, after his two fellow contenders had retired from the race, fortunately with only minor wounds to face and shins.

I'm happy to say we kept in close touch throughout his distinguished parliamentary career. He would often seek my advice over presentation, and I was only too happy to give it. For instance, in 1984, as Secretary of State for Transport he called me in to help butter up angry members of the Railusers Association who were distressed at the poor quality of service offered by British Rail. 'I thought I'd start my speech with something along the lines of "Piss off the lot of you, get off your fat arses, stop whining and why not buy yourselves a decent car if you hate the trains so much" – or do you think I should be a bit tougher with them, Wallace?' I told him that perhaps something like 'We are holding out great hopes for a radically improved service in the coming years,' might be more the ticket, and he went along with it, albeit grudgingly. Needless to say, the Railusers Association fell for it hook, line and sinker, Nick earned high praise for his emollient, far-sighted approach, and before you could say Jack Robinson he had been promoted to Secretary of State for the Environment.

At Environment, he found himself facing the heavily-bearded and besandalled Green Brigade, with their endless catalogue of pernickety demands for saving the world for future generations and so on. Over an excellent dinner of Dolphin Paté and Roulade of Endangered Species, he asked me what I thought of the first draft of his opening speech for the One World Environment Conference at the Barbican. I read it through with much interest before making my comment. 'Are you sure that kicking your speech off by saying, "If only all you lily-livered smartypants would have the common courtesy to drop down dead, you'd make my life one helluva lot easier" will be viewed as striking quite the right note of give-and-take?' I asked him. After some argument, he agreed to change it to, 'May I, on behalf of Her Majesty's Government, welcome you all here today, and assure you that we are all of us deeply committed to the future of this super planet', which, in the event, went down very well.

And so to last week's article on Good Manners. When I dropped into his office to help, he was thrilled to see me, elbowing four secretaries out of the way in order to shake my hand. 'I'm sick to bloody death with all this swearing,' he muttered, 'and everyone's so damn rude these days. Yesterday, I told an old lady to shove off and, d'y'know, she didn't even have the common courtesy to reply! Put these thoughts into decent English for me Wallace!'

'Only,' I replied, 'if you say "please".'

Of Bacon, Bubbles and Antelopes

THE POSITION OF THE ARTIST IN SOCIETY

Our story begins in the early 1970s (dread decade!). My old friend Lady Bubbles Rothermere, or Harmsworth as then was, phoned to tell me that she had heard of a marvellous new painter called Francis Sausage. Could I persuade him to paint a super portrait of her in her lovely new ballgown with her favourite peke, Fluffy-bun?

After some swift detective work, I realised that the artist to whom she referred was in all likelihood Francis Bacon. 'But would he be quite the man for you, Bubbles?' I asked her over the telephone. 'They say he's very poor at taffeta.' But she was not to be dissuaded. She had read in *Vogue* magazine that he was the master of modern angst and the dislocation of the human soul, and as she had been having a perfectly hellish time over the past fortnight with the soft furnishings department of Peter Jones, she thought Mr Sausage sounded just the ticket.

At that time, I was a director of Arnold Fine Art of Jermyn Street, an independent company devoted to 'extending the creative interflow of mutual understanding between art and industry' or, in layman's terms, extracting 50% commission from overworked businessmen for introducing them to suitably house-trained portraitists. Most of our clients were only too happy to take on any artist capable of easing a few inches off their waists with paintbrush and canvas, and of lending authoritative yet benevolent expressions to their faces.

But one or two of the more, shall we say, masochistic types, mustard-keen to sacrifice themselves to the cause of 'art'(!), demanded that their portraits be painted by louche, untrustworthy types who would doubtless allot them three eyes and two noses and then charge them an additional 75% for the extra work involved.

Of this genre, sponsored by Arnold Fine Art, perhaps the most memorable are *Lord Sainsbury Sitting On Sharp Thistle* by Lucian Freud (1974) *Lord Goodman Naked On Ironing Board* by John Bratby (1977) and *HRH Princess Margaret Bearing Putrid Eel* by R. B. Kitaj (1978), as well as the specially-commissioned black-and-white photographic sequence of the Conran Family by Diane Arbus (1971) simply entitled *Bleak*. I can't seriously pretend that any of them were very much to my taste, though I could appreciate the vivid blues and greens that went to make up Sir John Harvey-Jones's moustache in Gilbert and George's remarkable *Sir John in Snorkel and Flippers*, painted for the ICI Senior Executive Washroom in 1981.

I tracked Francis Bacon down to a fiercely bohemian haunt in Soho. Wheezing from the cigarette smoke that seemed to spout from every aperture, I approached the great artist, informing him of a client who would pay him handsomely for a full-length colour portrait to hang in her spacious Eaton Square drawing-room. 'Does she have a dead pig?' was Bacon's first response. I replied that she could undoubtedly get hold of one from Harrods. 'And I'll need a mutilated antelope too,' he added. And thus the deal was clinched.

Two months later, I received my invitation to Eaton Square 'For the grand unveiling of A New Portrait of Lady "Bubbles" Harmsworth by Mr Francis Sausage, RSVP.' Frankly, I welcomed the diversion, as I had been experiencing difficulty with a new portrait of Charles Forte by the Australian painter, Sidney Nolan. Sir Charles had fully expected to be portrayed sitting proudly in the refurbished Presidential Suite at the Five

Star THF Hotel on the outskirts of Droitwich. Imagine his distress on delivery of the finished painting to find himself portrayed strung up by the neck on a Giant Cactus in the outback near Alice Springs wearing nothing but a tin helmet and a pair of pink socks.

The gasps were audible at the grand unveiling of Lady Harmsworth's portrait, and for good reason. Bubbles was visible only as a screaming mouth floating in mid-air, the mutilated antelope and the dead pig hogging the rest of the canvas. But, somewhat to my surprise, she seemed thrilled with the finished product, delighted that the painter had removed all sign of unsightly dental fillings from her screaming mouth. I am reliably informed that Lady Rothermere's dentist has a reproduction of the painting on his waiting-room wall to this day, a splendid advertisement for the benefits of private dental care.

Mr John Birt

INCLUDING A CHOICE OF DELICIOUS HOT BEVERAGES

Might I shed some light on the events surrounding the appointment of Mr John Birt to the post of Director-General of the BBC? As one of the longest-standing Governors of that most venerable of institutions I think I may be permitted to throw secrecy to the winds.

I have long been a Birt man. I remember urging his appointment as Deputy Director-General back in 1987 against stiff opposition from my fellow Governors, who at that time included Lord Goodman, the delightful Dame Anna Neagle, leading industrialist Mr Peter Clowes, Birmingham hotelier Mr David Hunter and the much-loved Private Godfrey from the long-running television series *Dad's Army*.

As I remember it, the others were worried by my candidate's comparative lack of experience, but I was to argue most forcefully that his record at LWT was extraordinarily impressive: he was rumoured to have been at least partly responsible for creating the famous 'Nick-Nick' catchphrase that had made Mr Jim Davidson one of the best-loved comedians on the small screen; he revolutionised LWT's news and current affairs coverage by launching the highly successful *Blind Date* to replace it; he had attracted talent of the calibre of pocket-sized chanteuse Lynsey de Paul to lend new punch to religious programming; and he overturned all the old, outdated approaches to educational broadcasting by dropping it altogether. I was also immensely impressed by the dynamic and youthful design of his spectacles.

The public at large would, I felt, immediately fall for this 'loveable Charlie', whose charm owed so much to the popular character 'Doc Cox' of BBC's *That's Life*.

I first suspected that John's sheer commitment to broadcasting values might lead him to the very top when he arrived at Lime Grove complete with BBC news camera crew, personal publicist, mobile drinks cabinet and a selection of Pan's People all chanting his name. Then and there, I realised that his wholly admirable 'Mission to Expand' was well underway.

Within weeks, he had radicalised (dread word!) the news-gathering operation by awarding pop-up biros to every anchorman, training them to press them jauntily before returning them to their pockets as the lights dimmed at the end of each broadcast. John will probably be best remembered, however, for attracting from ITN two of the most outstanding newscasters of their day, whose names, alas, my secretary has temporarily mislaid.

I suppose poor Checkland should have seen it coming. While he was busying himself with the sums, young John would be entertaining the media to a choice of delicious beverages (hot/cold black/white sugar/no sugar) in the executive canteen. By the end of his first four years, articles galore were singing his praises, and the Governors – who now counted among their number the immensely distinguished old Mr Grace, Executive Director of Grace Brothers' Department Store – had greatly warmed to this resourceful young man.

After a doctor's certificate was produced confirming that two of my fellow Governors, who had ostentatiously abstained from voting for over three hours, had in fact been dead since the previous day, the vote swung towards a jubilant John. Like most of my fellow Governors, I have a tremendous aversion to the dread gogglebox(!), but I feel sure that it is now in the right hands, and may be safely ignored by one and all in the years to come.

Colonic Irrigation

IN DEFENCE OF THE DUCHESS OF YORK

I fear that faced with Miss (Ms!) Lynn Barber 'sounding off' (dread words!) on the page opposite we are none of us going to get much peace o'er our bacon, eggs and bangers upon a Sunday morn. Frankly, I ascribe that lady's desire for shocking and 'poking fun' to those far-off years when, as wife of Mr Heath's Chancellor of the Exchequer in the early Seventies (disagreeable decade!), she was expected to bottle up her emotions and keep smiling.

Still, there was little excuse in a family newspaper for Barber's unseemly revelations last week concerning the admirable Duchess of York. If the Duchess has indeed signed on for a course of 'colonic irrigation', that is strictly between her and her irrigators. I myself have made it perfectly clear from the start of this affair that I have not the slightest intention of prying into whatever may or may not go on in the sensitive area of the Duchess's rear quarters.

I am glad to note that other senior commentators have followed my lead. Bernard Levin, for instance, in his trenchant defence of Wagner last Wednesday, made only a passing reference to the revelations, comparing the final triumphant chorus of the assembled Valkyrie in *The Ring Cycle* to the 'glorious whoosh – at once cleansing and victorious – that one might expect to hear emerging through the door of the Duchess of York's specialist during a successful colonic irrigation'. Wisely, he ignored the matter entirely on Friday in his trenchant tour-de-force on apartheid, merely stating towards the end of a closely-argued piece that, in the new South Africa, comparatively minor issues such as compulsory seat-belts, restraints on tobacco advertising and the pros and cons of the colonic irrigation of the Duchess of York, would probably take low priority in the debating chamber.

That most sensitive yet forthright of opinion-formers, Mr Paul Johnson, has also seen fit to leave the issue tastefully to one side, urging readers to make up their own minds and to write to their MPs. In his only piece directly tackling the question, headed, 'An Entirely Private Matter', he argued persuasively that 'it is only too easy to pour cold water on the Duchess'. He then went on to suggest that forcible colonic irrigation could well hold the answer to the 'so-called joyriding, wanton vandalism and downright thuggery that is now rampant in our inner-cities. In future, the British Bobby on the beat must be armed with the very best anal syringe that the finest British craftsmanship can provide'.

In a more whimsical piece for *The Spectator*, Johnson defiantly wrote of other issues entirely. Previewing his forthcoming exhibition of watercolours, he revealed that 'the imagination of the watercolourist is instinctively drawn to the copse and the vale, to the play of sunlight upon water, to the ripple of wind through the wheat field and, in my own case, to the supreme visual pleasure of the colonic irrigation of one of the nation's most bonny young Duchesses.' He was otherwise at pains to avoid any mention of the matter.

My old *confrère* and quaffing partner Peter Jenkins, who keeps his ear well to the ground, revealed in our sister newspaper that 'sources close to Mr Major confirm that he has not yet ruled out the possibility of discussing with his Cabinet the colonic irrigation of the entire Royal Family'. Peter admitted that it was 'a vexed issue' which 'could not be swept under the carpet'.

However, he did not expect to see it on the Agenda at Maastricht, at least in the first few days.

Peter's rival columnist on *The Daily Telegraph*, Bill Deedes, devoted his Tuesday piece to an unashamedly nostalgic look at the enemas of days gone by. 'A lot of nonsense is talked these days about "class",' he began. 'Well do I remember the marvellous sense of community spirit that existed during the General Strike. People from all stations would pop into each other's houses after luncheon (or "dinner") and before dinner (or "tea") to offer one another colonic irrigation. In those far-off days of colonic camaraderie, it was still true to say that one's neighbour's enema was one's truest friend . . . ' I only hope that the tabloid press follows Bill's sensitive handling of this delicate matter in the weeks to come.

The Crystal Ball

A SEASONED POLITICAL PUNDIT ALLOWS HIMSELF
THE ODD BLAST ON THE OLD TRUMPET!

At this time of year, the temptation to blow one's own trumpet is to be firmly resisted, yet blow it one must. It is a time for political commentators to take stock of their predictions over the past year. Our regular readers are entitled to ask just how many came to pass.

On average I reckon to score a 95% success rate in my regular political columns. In 1990, I failed only in three comparatively minor areas – 'My Money's On Maggie for Ten More Years' (October, 1990), 'Heseltine's The Man' (November, 1991) and 'Major to Call Snap Election' (December, 1990). All my other predictions, from the purely social – 'Elizabeth Taylor to Remarry?' (February, 1990) – to the immensely important – 'Ulster Troubles may Continue for Some Time Yet' (March, 1990) – have about them the uncanny ring of prescience.

In 1991, my score was, if anything, rather higher. Looking through my leather-bound cuttings book, I note that in January I was the only commentator to predict a period of severe retrenchment in the Soviet Union. 'Let me tell you this,' I wrote in my 'Arnold at Large' column in *The Daily Mail*, 'and let me tell you this again. It will be many a long year before the city of Leningrad (unlike the proverbial big cat which sounds a bit like it!) changes either its spots – or indeed its name.' This prediction was true in all but essentials: the city of Leningrad may now be called 'St Petersburg', but I understand that most of the offices and domestic buildings remain in exactly the same places – making another bullseye for Arnold!

After a couple of near-misses in the spring – 'Major Favours April Election' (March, 1991), 'Sun and Surf: That's Yugoslavia!' (April, 1991) – I was well back in my stride by early summer, predicting, as I remember, an early end to the Gulf War – 'Iraq: America's Vietnam' (May, 1991) and, in my 'Arnold at Large' column, I had the courage to tackle Hard Left infiltration of the Shadow Cabinet – 'Nellist Set to Rout Hattersley for Deputy Leadership' (June, 1991).

If I may say so, one learns to feel the pulse of 'ordinary people' by keeping one's fingers firmly on the ground, and never being influenced by one's many close personal friendships with very senior politicians. This is how I first detected a great swing in public opinion behind Norman Lamont, a trend I first pinpointed shortly after he had invited me to holiday with him and his family on the Italian Riviera. It was then that I wrote 'Never before has a Chancellor – Tory or Labour – commanded so much respect and real affection from the ordinary bloke in the street. In pubs and on street corners, in the bowling alley and coffee bar, they are saying to one another "Good old Norm, he'll pull us through" ' ('Arnold at Large' May, 1991).

In the same way, my long experience of the real Soviet people, bless them, told me to maintain faith in their courage throughout the August coup, whatever their self-appointed 'leaders' might say. My trust ('Death of a Dream: The USSR Post-Glasnost' August, 1991) was confirmed when Gorbachev returned in triumph ('Gorby Comeback Halts Yeltsin' August, 1991). Just last week, I had cause to argue in my *Spectator* think-piece that Norman Lamont is the most suitable candidate to oversee the Russian economy at this delicate time in its history: we must wait to see whether history rises to my challenge.

As early as March, my pen and its influence had

turned to America. From a lifelong knowledge of and interest in that extraordinary country, I argued that Teddy Kennedy was gaining in stature every day, and that the Democratic nomination was now his for the asking. Later events served only to reinforce this judgement. I was also able to pooh-pooh – against the whims of my less cautious colleagues – any likelihood of an early release for the Western hostages in Beirut. Their subsequent release was, of course, the exception that proves the rule.

From the economic front ('MGN Shares Surefire Winner' September, 1991) to the world of entertainment ('Sir Peregrine to Join Chippendales' October, 1991), I have, it is fair to say, scored palpable hits time and time again. Let us hope that my luck and, let's be frank, good judgement continue to come up trumps in 1992 – The Year of Lamont.

Desert Island Discs

BUZZ ALDRIN OR DOROTHY SQUIRES?

Fifty years young! I refer, of course, to *Desert Island Discs* on the dear old Home Service, the brainchild of the immortal Roy Plomley. I am lucky enough to count myself one of the few people alive today of sufficient stature to have been featured twice, the first time with Roy himself, the second with my fellow broadcaster and quaffing partner Michael Parkinson, of whom more anon.

The story of how Roy came to think up the idea is now legend, but still merits repetition. One dark night, unable to get to sleep, Roy, at that time an out-of-work plagiarist down on his luck, was listening to the radio. Suddenly, a programme came on in which a celebrity chose his favourite eight records, plus a book and luxury item. The name of the programme – a name he never forgot – was *Desert Island Discs*. Roy listened spellbound. At daybreak, he reached for the telephone and dialled a trunk call to the leading radio impresario of the day. 'I've an idea for a long-running radio programme,' he said, 'by the name of *Desert Island Discs*.' And the rest, as they say, is now part of history (*A Concise History of Pilfered Ideas*, Routledge, 1986).

Roy's technique as an interviewer – a technique he learnt from close study of the great radio interviewers of the past – was that he, the interviewer, would ask the questions. Simple, but effective. He would then wait while the subject gave an answer before going on to ask another question, often entirely different. After half an

hour, he would say, 'Goodbye', thus neatly drawing the
programme to an end. His questions were direct and
unassuming, often disarming the interviewee with their
faux naiveté:

'I believe you first became famous as an astronaut
on the 1969 Apollo space mission,' he asked Dorothy
Squires, the leading warbler of the day.

'No,' she replied, a little testily.

'Ah,' replied Roy, 'I must be thinking of Buzz Aldrin,
next week's guest.'

Ever the pro, he got out of a tricky situation with
some deft footwork: 'But I imagine, like most people,'
he said, 'you dream of singing at Cape Canaveral?'

'Not at all,' she replied.

'Let's have your first record,' said Roy, thereby
deflating what might have turned into an awkward situation.

My own debut on *Desert Island Discs* took place in
May, 1971. I took pains to reflect my outgoing and
charming yet at times painfully shy, even complex,
character in my choice of records, and I was keen also
to stress my renowned sense of humour, though not at
the expense of my more maudlin and thoughtful side,
so that when Roy said, 'Your first record', I was able
to reply, 'Well, Roy, I have always been fond of anything by Russ Conway'. From there on it was plain
sailing all the way.

My second appearance was in 1986, under the watchful eye of the much-maligned Mr Michael Parkinson.
The two of us were old friends from way back, veterans
of countless charity fundraising events for that cause
close to both our hearts, The Lords Taverners. In one
summer alone, we had organised an expedition on a
fun-bus to take disabled children to tea at the Thame-
side home of Dickie Henderson. The money raised from
this expedition (each disabled child was charged £15 a
head, paper hats and sandwiches extra) was then
ploughed back into the sport, refurbishing the bar-cum-

lounge area in the Taverners' suite at Lords, a most worthwhile cause, and frankly long overdue.

Michael took a more relaxed and 'matey' approach than Roy had ever attempted, thus managing to shed light on my more magnetic and effervescent side. 'I guess you must have been something of a hit with the fairer sex in your time, eh, Wallace?' he asked me, and we both chuckled heartily while I recounted a saucy anecdote or three! Some have criticised Michael for taking the show 'downmarket' (35% of his chosen guests picked a pack of ribbed condoms as their luxury item, a further 54% chose 'Ernie: The Fastest Milkman in the West' by Benny Hill as their all-time favourite disc), but I would beg to disagree. To be frank, one of the greatest troubles facing today's presenter, Miss Lawley, is this: with Gilbert Harding, Mr Pastry and Mrs Mills no longer with us, where on earth can one find the true stars anymore? Look no further, Sue, look no further!

Farewell, Lime Grove

OF FYFE ROBERTSON, KATHY KIRBY AND DIXON OF DOCK GREEN

Might I add my own ha'penny'orth to the valedictions to Lime Grove, of blessed memory?

In the Fifties, when the magic lantern was still in its infancy, I was, of course, a senior presenter on the fast-moving *Good Evening* current affairs programme, which was later to shorten its title to *Evening* before a change of format under the name of *Evening Tonight* heralded a new, faster pace. *Evening Tonight*, you will remember, then split into two separate current affairs magazines, *Evening*, a fast-moving news-based half hour jointly hosted by Fyfe Robertson and the then Gerald Nabarro, and the celebrated *Tonight* with Cliff Michelmore, Kathy Kirby, my own good self and the then Woodrow Wyatt at the helm.

Tonight (later to become two very different shows, *Night*, a medium-paced current affairs programme hosted by Alan Whicker, and *Toni*, a fast-moving all-action thriller series set on the Italian Riviera, starring the young Peter Wyngarde) is now rightly praised as the precursor of such programmes as *World in Acton* – later to make the leap from local to national as *World in Action* – and, of course, *Panorama*, the BBC's flagship for fast-moving documentary features, presented by noted heavyweights such as Richard Dimbleby, Christopher Soames, Clare Rayner, Robert Morley and the young Cyril Smith.

Golden years, and an era now judged the most innovative in the history of broadcasting. At that time, Lime

Grove was a veritable hive of activity, buzzing with new ideas and revolutionary techniques. These days, it is hard to imagine the stir caused by such mould-breaking programmes as *Dixon of Dock Green*. I suppose that the young of today would now regard Jack Warner as a bit old hat, but to us at Lime Grove in the Fifties he was undoubtedly Britain's answer to Marlon Brando. Like Brando, Jack was steeped in the Method School, run by Miss Dorothy Method from her attractive home on the outskirts of Chiddingfold. He was thus able to bring a dynamic energy to his role as crimebuster PC George Dixon. For instance, it was Jack himself who changed his catchphrase, originally scripted as 'A Very Good Evening to One and All, and Special Greetings to Their Royal Highnesses Should They Be Viewing', to the more colloquial 'Evenin' All', amidst understandable upset among the powers that be.

I myself had a hand in scripting some of the more memorable episodes of *Dixon*, injecting them with a 'gritty realism' (dread phrase!) that was way ahead of its time, as can be witnessed in the following exchange from Episode 678, in which George Dixon cross-questions a suspect:

PC Dixon: Mmmm. Very nice cuppa tea, this.

Suspect: I didn't do it, guvnor, honest I never!

PC Dixon: Come on, son, here's a cuppa tea for you. You'll find it's very nice.

Suspect: Mmmm. You're right, guvnor. This *is* a very nice cuppa tea, is this. A very nice cuppa tea indeed.

PC Dixon: So tell me honestly, son – did you do it?

Suspect: Yes, guvnor. I done it. I'm a wrong 'un, and that's for sure. I blame it on me upbringing.

PC Dixon: Stuff and nonsense, son. *(To camera):* You know, it's surprising the difference a little chat over a nice cuppa tea can make when you're dealing with villains. We'll soon have that young bloke swingin' from the end of a good strong length of rope – but

not before he's had a nice cuppa tea! Evenin', all!
(Salutes. End.)

In current affairs presentation, too, I earned a reputation as a mould-breaker. In the heyday of *Good Evening*, I made a splash with this hard-hitting exchange on camera with Mr Macmillan, a scene discussed in hushed tones to this very day:

Wallace Arnold: Good evening, viewers. How did you enjoy your trip to Rhodesia, sir?

Mr Macmillan: Eh?

Wallace Arnold: How did you enjoy your trip to Rhodesia, sir?

Mr Macmillan: Not too bad, not too bad.

Wallace Arnold: Sunny?

Mr Macmillan: Yes, but not *too* sunny. Can't abide it *too* sunny, y'know.

Wallace Arnold: Absolutely not, couldn't agree more, sir. Cheerio, viewers . . .

This was the very first time on British television that a British Prime Minister had been subjected to such dogged questioning about a trip abroad. Of course, a terrific rumpus ensued, but we all felt that we had pushed forward the boundaries of television. These days, alas, the floodgates have opened and all manner of impertinence is committed in the name of 'investigative' journalism. Times change, but seldom, I fear, for the better.

Frankly Rather Common

The ever-beady eyes of Arnold have been much over-worked of late, I fear. On Thursday evening, shortly after dinner, they bore witness to the second episode of a new series on the dread gogglebox, *The Camomile Lawn*. Alas, within minutes they were twitching well nigh uncontrollably.

Have the Redbrick Rons who now populate the BBC no sense of how the upper classes behave? With mounting horror, I watched as one dreadful solecism followed head-over-heels upon another. No gent, for instance, has ever taken cream in his tea, yet there was Paul Eddington pouring away. Similarly, sunbathing to get brown is a recent craze of the middle-to-lower-middle classes, while napkins would never have been displayed in rings, and would most certainly not be referred to as – most dread of all words – *serviettes*.

My old quaffing partner Mr Philip Howard had sounded the alert in an important article in the previous week's *Times*, pointing out that gentlemen would never wear stick-up collars with black tie, nor eat at a table at which the pudding spoon and fork were positioned at the top of the place 'setting'. You may note that I have included inverted commas around his word 'setting' for, in all honesty, no gentleman would ever use such a word, a favourite of under-maids, journalists and what one might call the 'cleaning classes'. Nevertheless, Philip's conclusion was spot-on. 'Television dramas,' he wrote, 'are made by the shop assistant classes.'

Might I list one or two further howlers in *The Camo-mile Lawn* that poor Philip, for whatever reason (presumably breeding – or lack of!) failed to spot? In the late 1930s, the English (please, never *British*) upper classes would have rather died than have the lawns mown from left to right. Indeed, this rule gave birth to the phrase, highly popular at the time, 'He's a bit of a left-to-righter', to describe the encroaching *nouveaux riches*.

Again, the wooden leg worn by the Paul Eddington character afforded me a great deal of bother. In the 1920s and 1930s, it was considered an awful mistake within the upper echelons for a man who had lost a leg to be seen to replace it with a wooden leg. This is not to say that wooden legs could not be worn. Far from it: they could be worn, but only by those who already had two legs of their own. Indeed, in the early 1930s, the then Prince of Wales ensured that wooden legs became all the rage when he wore one to a party given by the Marquess of Bute in 1931. By the spring, Wooden Leg Parties were being thrown all over London, and it is said that Wallis Simpson originally caught the Prince of Wales's eye by wearing no less than *two* wooden legs – one on either side of her real legs – to a garden party at Knole. But no one-legged gentleman would ever be seen with a wooden leg, as my dear old friends Hoppety Metcalfe and Off-Balance Ogilvie would be the first to attest.

And why, may one ask, did the producers of *The Camomile Lawn* allow their female characters to be heard repeating, again and again, that awful word, *button*? 'I'll just do this button up, and then I'll be with you,' I heard one of them utter within the first ten minutes. It should go without saying that upper class women in the 1930s had been brought up never, under any circumstances, to employ such a word, and a fair amount of the social intercourse of that era was directed towards avoiding its mention, an awkward process as there was no ready alternative. To solve this linguistic problem, many of the grander houses would not allow their tailors to place buttons on any garment, which some historians suggest accounts for the rash of arrests for indecent exposure among the upper classes at the time.

A few final errors, if I may. In those days, no gentleman would have lived in a house overlooking the sea. The existence of the telephone was not acknowledged by the English upper classes until way into the 1960s, though some members were employing them as effective ice-cream scoops as early as the late 1940s. A proper lady would never have countenanced a croquet-hoop on the lawn, the splayed prongs being considered too suggestive for visiting tradesmen. Gentlemen have never worn swimsuits for bathing, preferring the warmer combination of jacket-and-tie. As we move inexorably towards our Classless Society, methinks we would do well to remember such things.

The Garrick Club

OUR DOORS REMAIN FIRMLY CLOSED TO THE
'UNFAIRER(!) SEX'

I am proud to say I have been a member of The Garrick
Club for twenty-three years, having been first proposed
for membership by Amis *père* and seconded by Worsthorne, who had himself been elected a member in
acknowledgement of ten years noble service on the
door, collecting hats, bidding gentlemen a very good
night and so forth, all with his customary aplomb. Few
would now realise that he was once a plumber's mate
from Catford. As I have long maintained, membership
of the Garrick does much for a man.

At that time, the question of electing women – or
what I rejoice to term 'the unfairer sex', bless their
scatty little heads! – had never arisen, though there had
been the odd eyebrow upturned upon the election of
Mr Melvyn Bragg, with his 'mop-top' hairstyle, and the
suspicion of a blow-dry. (On this latter point, the Garrick is a very broad church, and when it was heard that
Melvyn was an enthusiastic (if somewhat secretive!)
member of Lloyds he was admitted at once, soon rising
to the post of Secretary of the Junior Commonroom,
with joint responsibility for bins and stacking chairs.)

I first heard the idea mooted of admitting the beskirt-
ed fraternity some time in the mid-Seventies (dread
decade!) by Mr (later General) Manuel Noriega, at that
time an aspirant man of letters scraping a living writing
about the delicate early novels of Barbara Pym for the
literary magazines, later to make his name as something
of a big noise in Panamanian politics. As is now well

known, Noriega had something of an eye for the lasses, and had already made extensive plans to turn the ground floor dining room of The Garrick into an all-night discotheque featuring the hit sounds of Mr Barry White.

Frankly, the idea never got off the ground. Instead, it was quashed overnight by the Club Committee. After an Emergency All-Night meeting, the ruling was issued that not only were females not to be admitted as Members, but that Members were henceforth not permitted to wear dresses even in the Billiards Room – with the exception of a handful of the General Management Committee, and then only on production of a valid Doctor's Certificate.

With so many elderly gents of a theatrical persuasion enlisted as members in The Garrick, this draconian ruling was destined to cause a major obstruction, particularly in the period around Christmas and New Year, that seasonal hotbed of the Great British Pantomime. During a single Christmas period, an average of fifty Garrick Club members might be playing the Dame in a variety of pantos from Wimbledon to Walsall. Needless to say, they would all expect to be able to pop into their Club for a quick nip between shows or at week-ends without being required to change into more formal attire.

One Christmas, soon after the edict had been passed, I recall seeing Donald Sinden fresh from Mother Goose sitting at one end of the bar dressed in orange and pink dayglo polka-dot blouse with full frilly camiknicker *assemblage*, and at the other Sir Robin Day, having hotfooted it from the Tuesday matinee at the London Palladium (where he was appearing in 'Dick Whittington' with Freddie and the Dreamers, Rod Hull and Emu and the consistently under-rated Reg Varney) resplendent in spotty frock and comical hat. Next to them sat my old friend and quaffing partner Sir Nicky Fairbairn

MP, resplendent in the kilt and sporran of the Black Watch.

At that point my old friend and quaffing partner Woodrow Wyatt made an entrance, his distinctive face just visible over the bar. Woodrow is something of a traditionalist, and I had expected him to berate Day and Sinden for flouting the new dress regulations of the club. Not so. He placed one arm around Nicky and the other around Robin, pulled the cigar from his mouth with a theatrical flourish, and said, 'You three lovely ladies look as if you could manage a glass of bubbly with your old Uncle Woodrow!'

The consequences were far-reaching: an ambulance was called, the heavily-bandaged Wyatt transferred his membership to Boodles' and, in the long term, no women's clothing was worn ever again in the snug bar of The Garrick. O Tempora, O Mores!

THE GATHERING STORM

The Fifties: Decade of Disillusion

Wallace Arnold: Welcome to my Wireless. Welcome to my World. That's a catchphrase you've been hearing from me on your wireless for nearly four decades now, believe it or not! And the first of those decades was the Fifties. As is so often the case with decades, the Fifties got off to a flying start. Only later did they end in tears.

In 1951, that most agreeable – if raucous! – of musicals *South Pacific* had opened in London to ecstatic notices. Then, just two short years later, on June 1st, 1953, the news came through that Sir Edmund Hillary had conquered Everest for Britain – and all this on the eve of the Coronation of Her Majesty Queen Elizabeth II!

At the time of the Coronation, I was a young man, fresh down from Oxford, keen as mustard to make my way in Literary London. Imagine my exultation, then, when first I was contacted by Mr Godfrey Talbot of the BBC. The great man asked me if I would care to have a bash at commentating to the nation for a few minutes on the big day itself. If so, would I come without delay in full dress uniform to the Royal Broadcasting Training Centre in Aldershot. There all of us young whippersnappers – Robin Day, Alistair Burnett, Reg Varney, and yours truly, Wallace Arnold – were taught to speak slowly and clearly and with all due solemnity. But above all we were taught to speak *backwards*.

Let's listen to a snatch of that very first wireless broadcast of mine. As a mere novice, my job was to commentate on the thirty seconds or so it took the frail young Princess Lilibet to climb up the steps into her carriage, the carriage from which, just a few short hours later, she would emerge a queen. Needless to say, I was a huge success. Note particularly the skill with which I speak back-to-front, so important in conveying one's reverence for the great Royal pageant as it unfurled before a grateful nation:

(Sound of crackly radio, tuning noises, cheers in the background, perhaps a little neighing and whinnying. The young Wallace speaks.)

Wallace: Into her gold carriage, a carriage pulled by six horses, majestic as . . . um . . . um . . . majestic as only horses, six in number, can be, majestic and extra-ordinarily . . . um . . . horse-like, their manes noble in the sparkling sunlight, a bright, glorious June sunlight that through the clouds still struggles to appear, steps, bravely smiling but nervous perhaps a little, in her dignity resplendent, in her majesty triumphant, the Princess, young and fragile, to cheers tumultuous from the crowds surrounding. Godfrey you to over.

(Sound of more cheers and clip-clops)

*

Wallace Arnold: Golden days indeed, and the terrific sense of occasion I brought to bear on that historic pageant has ensured me a long and, I like to think(!), much-loved career on the wireless ever since.

Just three short years later, my wireless career received an unexpected uplift with the death of the French artist Raoul Dufy in 1955. Frankly, this was not something that would normally have bothered one a great deal, tragic though it undoubtedly was for the artist concerned and his immediate family. But today I pay tribute to Raoul Dufy's tragic demise as it marked for me an important step in my broadcasting career, lending much-needed zip to my first appearance on the Home Service's long-running and much-loved programme, *Any Questions*:

*

(Crackles of radio; we tune into Any Questions *in mid-sentence of the preceding panellist)*

Conservative MP: . . . and I see no reason whatever why capital punishment, humanely administered, shouldn't be followed by a few swift strokes of the birch . . .

(Tumultuous cheering and applause)

Chairman: And our next question please, from a young lad of, I think, just 11 years of age.

John Major-Ball: John Major-Ball aged 11 from South London. What are the panel's thoughts on the recent death of the prominent French artist Raoul Dufy?

Chairman: Wallace Arnold?

Young Wallace: Like most Britons, my only thoughts are how on earth to pronounce the name of the poor fellow!!

(Laughter and applause)

Young Wallace: Ray-Owl? Duff-Yer?

Isobel Barnett: Rule Duff Y?

Conservative MP: Rolf Doolally?

Gilbert Harding: Rolled Up Duffle?

(Laughter and applause)

Chairman: Well, that should give you plenty to choose from, questioner! Many thanks there to Wallace Arnold. And our next questioner please!

Peregrine Worsthorne: Peregrine Worsthorne. Plumber's mate from Catford. Does the panel agree with me that the new contraption known as television is little more than just a passing fad?

(Fades)

*

Wallace Arnold: In retrospect, it is possible to date the death of Raoul Dufy as the great watershed event of the postwar era. That historic *Any Questions* broadcast was the first time the vast majority of Britons had ever heard an artist discussed in any depth on the wireless. But it was not to be the last. Less than a year later, on May 10th, 1956, the young John Osborne produced a stage-show without music called *Look Back in Anger* which opened at The Royal Court Theatre. From then on, the decade went into swift decline. No less a personage than the Duke of Edinburgh was soon blown off his feet by the prevailing wind of revolution and just two short years later, in 1958, he ensured that the last debutantes were presented to the Queen at Buckingham Palace. Things would never be the same again. Suddenly, to get on in British life one had to be young, angry and an artist. From my own point of view, obviously one had to adapt and survive. By 1957, along with Kingsley Amis, Acker Bilk, John Osborne, Colin MacInnes and Tommy Steele, the name of Wallace Arnold had become synonymous with British Youth and Rebellion. Witness, for instance, this wireless interview I granted the young John Freeman:

*

(Radio crackles. Face to Face *theme music)*

John Freeman: Wallace Arnold, you have been described as 'the original Angry Young Man', yet only five years ago as an Oxford graduate you were only too happy to pay tribute to the sovereign in the wireless broadcast of the Coronation. Would you describe yourself now as angry?

Young Wallace: A little miffed from time to time.

John Freeman: What angers you most?

Young Wallace: It's the little things in life. Sloppy service in restaurants. The unscrubbed neck. The unshined shoe. Those who attack the policies of the Conservative Government without bothering their little heads about coming up with a viable alternative.

John Freeman: You and Kingsley Amis have been described as England's answer to The Beat Generation.

Young Wallace: Quite so, we're very much the Eat Generation. We just love a good meal out. Steak and french fries – *must* one call them chips? Sautée pots. Bottle or two of half-way decent wine. Nothing better. Recently, we've been gathering in smokey clubs to recite our favourite recipes from the works of Elizabeth David, bit of sax in the background, that sort of thing. Then it's early nights all round for a healthy start in the morning with a Full English Breakfast and lashings of hot coffee.

*

Wallace Arnold: Youth. What an appalling word it now seems. Yet in 1957, *tout le monde* seemed to want, to use the dreadful jargon of the time, to 'Swing to its Beat'. The previous year had seen the emergence of those youthful swingers Bill Haley and The Comets in the frenetic feature film, *Rock Around the Clock*, a topic much discussed on numerous editions of *Any Questions* at the time:

*

Chairman: Might I now turn to the Reverend David Jenkins, who has created something of a stir with his controversial new book, *Jesus Wore Jeans*. Reverend Jenkins, we have here a young man from the armed forces, Private Ronald Ferguson, who wants to know where you stand on the new film, *Rock Around the Clock*. Do you feel, as he does, that it might have a deleterious effect on our young people?

Reverend Jenkins: 'Q the Op' as my many young friends would say.

Chairman: 'Q the Op'?

Reverend Jenkins: Sorry! *Quite the opposite.* I know an awful lot of what, for want of better words, we call young folk – and let me say straightaway that I'm a great believer in young folk, and also in the old, incidentally – and let's not forget those of us who are in between, or 'middle-aged', and then of course there are those caught in those awkward years between what one might call youth and middle age, not to mention those people – both men and women – who are, well, not old exactly but not middle-aged either – but to return, if I may, to the question, I know a lot of young folk who have been to see the splendidly energetic *Rock Around the Clock* and have been *deeply moved* by what they have seen. In a very real sense, it is a *deeply religious* film. I wonder if any of your listeners remember that marvellous last line, 'We're going to rock, going to rock, around the clock tonight'? Well, what was it that the Bible says that other young tearaway, Jesus Christ, said to Peter? 'Thou art for want of a better word Peter, and upon this *rock* I shall build, or at any rate construct, my church or community hall'. In other words, Jesus himself was saying *rock around the clock*! all those millions of years ago. Yes, tremendously exciting.

Chairman: Our next questioner please: Dr Bodkin Adams?

*

Wallace Arnold: In the spring of '57, I was approached by the Light Programme to pioneer the wireless's very first 'pop' music show. It was to be the first of many manoeuvres to attract more 'young people' to the wireless, manoeuvres, I might add, successfully out-witted today by my own presence in this delightfully arcane series of off-the-cuff reminiscences!

By a stroke of luck, I was given a free rein to hand-pick my fellow presenters, so I chose the acerbic and plain-speaking – some might say downright brash! – David Jacobs and, just before he took up a seat in the House of Commons, the famous 'Bexley Boy' himself, as famous then for his quiff and his winkle-pickers as he was later to become for his sailing and his chuckle – the inimitable Mr Edward Heath.

Of course, the convention of the time dictated that we present *Wallace Arnold Says it's Time for Smashing New Tunes* in full dinner jacket and bow tie but, believe me, we, to use the jargon of the time, 'sure put on the style'!

Just listen to this extract in which Ted Heath and I interview that rising young singing star on the American scene, Mr Elvis Presley, on what turned out to be his only visit to the United Kingdom:

*

(Fading extract of 'Rock with the Caveman' by Tommy Steele)

Young Wallace: And now, youngsters, I am delighted to say that we have a discussion with the man who's already being billed as America's Answer to Tommy Steele – Mr Elvis Presley! Ted?

Young Ted Heath: Thank you, Wallace. Thank you very much indeed. Well, Mr Priestland, we're delighted to be able to welcome you to the studio today, very delighted indeed I must say. Wallace?

Young Wallace: They tell me you have high hopes of teaching our own Tommy Steele a thing or two! So watch out, Tommy, if you're tuned into us today!

Seriously though, we're delighted to have you in the studio for this chat today, Elvis.

Young Ted Heath: Absolutely delighted.

Young Wallace: And fingers crossed that you don't give Tommy Steele too many sleepless nights!

Young Ted Heath: Quite.

Young Wallace: Well, I'm afraid that's all we've got time for! Many thanks to Elvis Presley for coming in to talk to us.

Young Ted Heath: Many thanks indeed.

Young Wallace: And so let's close tonight's show with another super Tommy Steele waxing. I must be careful not to drop this one because it's called, yes, 'Butterfingers'!

(Fade out on extract from 'Butterfingers' by Tommy Steele)

Wallace Arnold: The Fifties had seen the discovery of the Teenager with all his attendant loud music, sloppy lifestyle and casual devil-may-care attitudes, a discovery from which this country has still not fully recovered. Looking back on the Fifties from a distance of some thirty-odd years with Dr Anthony Clare during my famous 1989 appearance on *In the Psychiatrist's Chair*, I was brave enough to reveal just something of the emotional scars still embedded in my psyche by that Dread Decade:

*

Dr Anthony Clare: So, Wallace, behind that assured and thrusting youth of the Fifties, there was – correct me if I'm wrong – another Wallace Arnold, perhaps less secure, more nervous, struggling to get out?

Wallace Arnold: Yes. *(pause, chokes)* Yes. Forgive me. By late 1959, I suddenly felt that everything had gone too far. The hula-hoop. The transistor radio. The Bubble Car. Frozen Peas. They were all getting on top of me. All too, too much *(chokes)*.

Dr Anthony Clare: Anything else?

Wallace Arnold: Yes . . . Even now I find it hard to say the awful word. Stupid, really, I suppose.

Dr Anthony Clare: Not at all . . .

Wallace Arnold: SLACKS. That's it. SLACKS. Women in SLACKS. Couldn't take them. Really I couldn't. *(Breaks down)* Slacks, slacks, slacks . . .

Dr Anthony Clare: There, there. Deep breath. Big blow. *(Sound of Wallace Arnold blowing nose)* All better.

*

Wallace Arnold: But worse was to follow. As midnight struck on December 31st, 1959, the Fifties were to usher in that most dread of decades, the Sixties, an era I shall be explaining in full next week. Until then, this is Wallace Arnold saying, 'Welcome to my Wireless. Welcome to my World'.

The Gettysburg Address

CECIL AND MARGARET AND PETERS AND LEE

From small acorns mighty oaks doth grow, as the Immortal Bard put it. I can't tell you how delighted I am that my own little acorn of an idea – that Mrs Thatcher (or Lady Thatcher as we must learn to call her!) might record Abraham Lincoln's Gettysburg Address – has come to flower.

She is, of course, a recording natural, taking to it like the proverbial winged biped to H_2O. She recited the Gettysburg Address all in one take, even adding a few impromptu words of her own on her role in the historic Falklands victory, plus one or two strong words against the ill-fated treaty of Maastricht. As we had the recording 'in the can' (dread expression!) in just seventeen minutes and we had booked the recording studio and orchestra for the full hour, we decided to waste not a second, and before you could say 'Jacques Delors' we had set about cutting a few more discs, as we say in the industry(!).

Looking around the studio for any sheet music that might be to hand, I chanced upon a cache of classic hit tunes from the Sixties and Seventies, including 'Welcome Home' by the immortal Peters and Lee and 'Seaside Shuffle' by Terry Dactyl and the Dinosaurs, a song which did so much to enliven the Hit Parade back in the summer of 1972. (Oddly enough, 'Terry Dactyl' was later revealed to be a pseudonym for my old friend and quaffing partner Mr Kenneth Baker, whose political career was then, as now, somewhat in the doldrums.

Rumour has it that he is now hoping to revive his old group for a one-off recording, possibly of the great Christmas classic, 'I'm Only a Poor Little Sparrow', but this is all strictly *entre nous*.)

Of the sheet music available, Margaret was best acquainted with Peters and Lee's 'Welcome Home'. This, in turn, led to a problem: if Margaret was to take the female vocal (Lee), then who on earth was to be male (Peters)? There was no time at all to send out for a professional vocalist – Margaret's own favourite, Andy Williams, say, or our own Val Doonican – and so, with only half an hour of recording time left, we decided to search the extensive Abbey Road premises for an effective substitute.

Many people fail to realise that Abbey Road houses not just one recording studio but quite a number. As luck would have it, in the next door studio, Margaret's old colleague Cecil Parkinson – looking marvellously relaxed in a casual lime-green one-piece zip-up jogging suit with light floral cravat – had dropped in to cut the first few tracks on his forthcoming album of great Martin Luther King speeches (backed by the King's Singers and the London Symphony Orchestra, conductor Norrie Paramour).

'Wallace!' beamed Cecil, lifting his headphones gently off his head and giving his nicely-manicured hair a quick one-two with the old comb. 'What brings you to these parts? You're not working on old Enoch's album of Non-Stop Old Tyme Singalong Songs by any chance?'

'No' quoth I.

'Then it must be Norman Fowler's version of 'Young Gifted and Black', out soon on CD and cassette?'

'Not at all,' quoth I.

'Cecil,' I said, 'I'm on the big one. It's Margaret, it's Abraham Lincoln and it's *dynamite*.'

'Sounds smashing,' enthused Cecil, 'and how can I help?'

With the seconds ticking away, I swiftly explained

the position to Cecil. As luck would have it, 'Welcome Home' turned out to be one of his personal favourites, his good lady wife Ann having sung it to him to a banjo accompaniment on his return from late-night Parliamentary sittings in the Seventies (dread decade!) and early Eighties. A further stroke of luck ensued: Cecil had come equipped with his own dark glasses in the top pocket of his jumpsuit. When donned, they lent him an authentic look of the genial Peters, who, you will remember, had made them something of a personal hallmark.

Needless to say, the session went like a dream. Frankly, I doubt whether that mercurial creature, Joe Public, will notice the subtle variations wrought on the original by Margaret. 'Welcome Home, Welcome! / Come on in, and close the door / This is your Queen / Urging NO to Monsieur Delors'. I wonder if you, the more sophisticated *Independent on Sunday* reader, can spot 'em? Happy hunting!

Mr Graham Greene

And still I grieve for my old friend and quaffing partner Graham Greene, that veritable master of the written word. A true friend, a terrific admirer of my life and works, an obsessive reader of the many letters and books I sent him, his affection for me will live on in my mind.

I have written before of this essentially private man, so wedded to secrecy that he would allow only two journalists at a time into his flat in Antibes for exclusive interviews, and then only on Tuesdays and Thursdays. (It is, incidentally, often reported that Graham did not care to show his face on the dread gogglebox. However, my researchers tell me that this is in fact quite wrong: he appeared twice on *Juke Box Jury* in the mid-Sixties under the watchful eye of David Jacobs, the first time with Cilla Black, Lonnie Donnegan and Tommy Steele, the second with Peter Noone, Lulu and Bruce Forsyth; once on *Criss Cross Quiz* in 1963, achieving full marks in the third round; once on *Blue Peter* in 1964, assisting veteran presenter Christopher Trace as chief stoker on a traction engine; once on *Tonight* in 1965, to argue the toss about communism with the splendid Fyfe Robertson; and he also made a fleeting appearance in November 1968 on ATV's long-running *Crossroads* as the mysterious 'Lord Mulliver', who claimed to be the first husband of the redoubtable Miss Amy Turtle).

I raise the subject of the great Greene once again as I have been much struck by a distinguished article in this week's *Times Literary Supplement* entitled, 'The marginalia of Graham Greene'. It would appear that Greene's library is soon to be sold, and that several of the dusty tomes therein contained, many presented to him by his fellow authors, are furnished with that scrupulous scrivener's own hand-written comments, be they good, bad or indifferent!

I met the great man only once, at a cocktail party thrown by the late Bubbles Rothermere in the late Fifties. From that brief exchanged glance we struck up an immediate *rapport*, twin souls startled into mutual recognition through the hubbub and banter of a raucous soirée. The very next day, I placed my newly-published comical riposte to the female of the species, *The Unfairer Sex: Birds of the Unfeathered Variety* into an envelope, inscribed it, 'To Graham Greene: Friend, Mentor, Quaffing-Partner' and posted it to his modest digs in Nice. The silence that followed spoke volumes: Greene seemed instinctively to recognise me as his natural ally in the world of letters.

Needless to say, when my next book appeared – *Ahoy There Me Hearties! The Punch Book of Life On The Ocean Waves, edited by Wallace Arnold* – I posted it without delay to The Master, inscribing it with an affectionate, not to say wry!, 'Saucy Salutations to an old Sea Salt – from his Great Friend and Fellow Yarn-Spinner, Wallace A.' Once again, Graham took care not to respond to this presentation with anything so verbose as a card or letter: he was, after all, the master of the unspoken, and between two such soul-mates mere words seemed but flimsy things.

From that point on, our friendship secure, I posted the great man each of my tomes as and when they were published, including *If It's Wednesday, It Must Be Europe! – Wallace Arnold's Book Of The Great British Tourist* (1965), *Pardon My Aspidistra! – Arnold on Gardening* (1975), *Of Hedgerows and Hyacinths: The Collected Poems of Wallace Arnold* (1983), *Norman*

Fowler: The Man and the Myth (biography) (1988), and, of course, my recent *Pass the Port, Percival!: 500 Ice-breaking Anecdotes for the After-Dinner Speaker* (1989). I delighted to think of the celebrated author, tired from a hard day's penmanship, relaxing in bed with his favourite Arnold tome, thereby gaining a few chuckles and/or words of wisdom before lights out.

I now have the Auction Catalogue to The Library of the Graham Greene in front of me. Between 'Amis, K – with marginalia' and 'Austen, J – fully annotated' is listed 'Arnold, W., 15 volumes, 1959–89, all pristine condition, still sealed in original packaging'. Flattering, indeed, that the great man chose not to muddy my tomes with his inky pen, preferring to savour them unread! Those wishing to read up on this subject should consult my new volume *Arnold and Greene: A Literary Friendship* (Hutchinson, £14.99).

Lord Hailsham

AN ABOMINABLE CALUMNY

I have nothing but the very deepest respect for my old friend and quaffing partner Quintin Hailsham, and it was with unmixed delight that I found myself perusing the leaves of his estimable work of autobiography, *A Sparrow Brain*, published by Messrs Collins at the far-from-unreasonable price of £17.50.

I first bumped into Quintin at the 1957 Tory Party Conference in Brighton. But a young man, no doubt a little green around the gills, I was determined to further the lot of the ordinary working bloke by throwing my weight behind the more congenial elements in the Conservative Party. Perambulating along the front one day, I caught sight of the unmistakable figure of Quintin, clad in the eye-catching uniform of the Fairground Barker, awarding free candy floss and novelty items to all who signed a round-robin supporting his candidature for the post of Tory Party Treasurer.

I knew at once that I was in the presence of a first-rate mind. 'My mind,' he told me as we shook hands, 'is absolutely first-rate.' Pledging my support, and receiving in return a clockwork fieldmouse of a type one rarely encounters these days, I told myself that here was the leader for whom our great party had been waiting. 'I am the leader for whom our great party has been waiting,' he confirmed, as if reading my mind. I strode purposefully back to my hotel in a glow of contentment, occasionally turning back to see this forceful, highly intelligent man performing balancing acts with china plates on his nose for the assembled cameras.

We renewed our brief acquaintance at Blackpool the following year. Dressed as Snow White, posing proudly with a handful of first-rate dwarfs, he was holding a press conference to announce his appearance in the annual Tory charity pantomime, and to hit back at a malicious whispering campaign that he was in some way a self-publicist. 'That is the most abominable calumny circulated by odious and execrable mischief-makers,' he proclaimed to a peal of trumpets before exiting stage left, borne aloft by a pantomime horse.

By 1963, I had become Quintin's Man Friday, with responsibility for policy documents, travel arrangements, foreign liaison, make-up, costumes, and so on. It was in the very week of the party conference that Harold (Macmillan) announced his resignation as Prime Minister. Determined to avoid all charges of self-promotion, Quintin at once sent for his wife and child. He was then photographed by the gentlemen of the press in a variety of poses 'about the house' so as to emphasise his unassuming domesticity. Alas, he mistook the Hoover for a microphone and, attempting to perform a hearty medley of old Andrews Sisters favourites, he found his nose sucked headlong into the pipe, causing the 'photo-opportunity' to be switched to a nearby hospital.

Overlooked as Party Leader, he sought succour in a season of song and dance at the De La Warr Pavilion, Bexhill, where he delighted audiences nightly with his comical impressions of the farmyard. Slowly but surely, he built on this skill and the rest, as they say, is history.

Happier Times

King George VI and his wife, now the Queen Mother, were never any trouble at all. As is by now well-known, my father acted as their unpaid Press Attaché, a job that required no more than a couple of hours work every other year.

'LARGE CROWDS ASSEMBLE TO CHEER THEIR MAJESTIES' was, at that time, such a popular headline that at one point the *Daily Express* ran it three times in one week, with each edition a sell-out.

In the mid-Thirties, of course, there had been what one might describe as 'a little local difficulty' with King Edward VIII and his divorced American ladyfriend, name best forgotten, but the British Press had acted throughout with a scrupulous regard for the demands of propriety. Indeed, it was not until 1946, ten years after the King's abdication, that Beaverbrook's mighty *Daily Express* acknowledged – in a short paragraph towards the bottom of page 5 – that King Edward VIII was not still on the throne. At first, they had kept mum so as to avoid any possibility of scandal, and throughout the war they had maintained a similar silence so as not to dampen the morale of our fighting forces, strongly hinting for a good three years that a marriage between His Royal Highness and Miss Vera Lynn was on the cards.

Looking back on it, I now think that the great watershed years for the Royal Family came in the Sixties (dread decade!). The old Gentlemen of the Press had retired, and decent, cheerful, positive headlines that had served both nation and sovereign so well, such as 'QUEEN MOTHER'S SMILE AGAIN RADIATES OVER HER GRATEFUL PEOPLES THROUGHOUT THE WORLD' and 'PRINCE PHILIP SET TO CELEBRATE 37TH BIRTHDAY IN EIGHT DAYS TIME' and 'SMILING QUEEN ENJOYS "DELICIOUS" LIGHT LUNCH BEFORE TAKING SHORT WALK' now ceased to be printed. This, one remembers with a shudder, was the era of 'Flower Power', 'Pot Sniffing' and licentious musicals such as *Half a Sixpence*, a time when long-cherished values were thrown overboard, when businessmen slouched to work wearing T-shirts and suede shoes and humming tunes by Herman's Hermits, and when the *Sunday Telegraph* appointed a Deputy Editor named Peregrine. Society would never be the same again.

It was when Princess Margaret-Rose chose to marry a photographer called Jones that I began to realise that even the Royal Family was not immune to the prevailing trend. My father's days as Press Attaché to the Palace were by now coming to an end. He simply could not keep up with the fast-changing *mores* of the decade, and continued to issue strong denials of this particular Royal Engagement until a full two weeks after the marriage had occurred. He was one of the old school, strong in his belief that the general public was a creature which did not wish to be told all the gruesome details; at the time of the marriage of Princess Elizabeth to her Greek husband he had even argued for a press embargo, to be over-ruled only by instructions from the very top. He handed in his notice, with much regret, on the day in 1969 when Princess Anne attended the hippy-musical, *Hair*, clad in a purple one-piece trouser suit. Frankly, I believe he never really recovered from that last, great shock.

I took up the reins of the job soon after. The Press, once so discreet, had begun their downward slide into curiosity and sheer nosiness. My first major crisis occurred in 1974, when Princess Anne chose to accept Captain Mark Phillips's hand in marriage. True to my father's memory, I advised a media blackout, but was over-ruled by The Duke of Edinburgh, who had begun to get something of a taste for personal publicity. Needless to say, once the Press had been given an inch, they began to crave their mile, ringing up day and night with impertinent requests for, say, the Queen Mother's favourite colour, or questions relating to the favourite food of the young Prince Edward. When, in 1977, Princess Margaret-Rose officially separated from the photographer Jones, I stupidly trusted the Gentlemen (!!) of the Press to keep the news under their collective hats until a decent period of time – say, twenty-five years – had elapsed. Instead, they chose to emblazon it in front-page headlines so that, by the end of that day, every Tom, Dick or Harry on the Clapham Omnibus was aware of the personal tragedy that had befallen the sister of the Sovereign. Ahead loomed grim days indeed.

Mr Eric Heffer

MEMORIES OF A CROSS-PARTY QUAFFING PARTNER

It was with very great personal sadness that I heard of the demise of my old friend and quaffing partner, Mr Eric Heffer. The doughty champion of so many a just cause, he will be much missed by all those in the Tory Party who appreciate honesty, humility and great good humour in a politician, quite regardless of the cut of his politics.

Eric and I became firm friends in the early Seventies, after I had written an affectionate piece in the *Daily Mail* under the heading of, as I remember it, 'The Fat Oaf of the Hard Left'. In this piece, I argued that though Eric had a great many personal charms ('Let us not be mealy-mouthed. This man represents all that is bleak and selfish in our nation today. He must be stopped. And stopped quickly.') he was not, in a purely political sense, the best person to run affairs of state at that particular time.

There followed an – occasionally heated! – correspondence with Eric (dear, working-class, Eric), good-humouredly complaining to the Press Council of what he endearingly termed my 'fascist and totally unscrupulous character assassination'. Though we differed politically, we remained on the very best of terms as friends and colleagues. 'Let me buy you a pint, Eric,' I would say whenever I bumped into him in Annie's Bar. 'Up your arse,' he would joshingly reply, and I would laugh merrily in return, delighted to revel in his solid, old-fashioned, splendidly and unashamedly proletarian (dread word!) repartee before absenting myself for a bottle of claret with high-level Tory chums.

Over the years, I don't suppose we ever agreed on much. I had occasion to differ with him over the economy ('let us not be led by this Soviet-style commissar into further pussy-footing with the hard men of the Unions'), the Militant Tendency ('only an ugly old buffoon would choose to tango with these long-haired enemies of society') and the Gibraltar killings ('this blinkered apologist for terrorism deserves to be clapped in irons and pilloried by all right-minded folk'), but I always respected his deeply-held convictions, and the intellectual rigour and integrity he brought to all debate.

No doubt you will have read my small tribute to this great 'bloke' – for he never pretended to be anything other than a 'bloke' – in the obituary columns of last week's *Daily Telegraph*. 'Might I add a word to your excellent tribute to my old friend and quaffing partner Eric Heffer?' I began.

Eric had long held me in the very greatest respect, valuing my firmly-held opinions and the forthright manner with which I expressed them. Though he never said as much – we rarely found the time to speak to one another – he was, I would say, an old-style Socialist, properly deferential to his social superior, maintaining a firm belief in law and order, privatisation and decisive management of the NHS. An old Labour man, he held Mrs Thatcher in the highest regard, and I remain convinced that he secretly believed that the Conservative Party could – and should – win the next election.

Methinks we shall not see his like again.

Mr Michael Heseltine

THE WORLD BEYOND *BLUE PETER*

Perchance I have already penned a small memoir of my old friend and quaffing partner Michael Heseltine's years as a *Blue Peter* presenter, deputising for Mr Christopher Trace, before, with brilliant timing, ousting him from his job.

Now seems a perfect time to continue these reminiscences of Michael's rise to fame and fortune. Frankly, *Blue Peter* was not big enough to contain his myriad ambitions. I first realised this when, passing through the Peter Jones television department at 4.45 on a damp Thursday afternoon in – what? '63? '64? – I chanced to see Michael's striking features echoing all about me in row upon row of dread goggleboxes. Moving closer – I had promised myself a Shetland woolly, and felt that closer scrutiny of said garment on the Boy Heseltine might pay dividends – I couldn't help but notice that Michael had interrupted his useful introduction to the story of King Alfred and the Cakes with a vehement denunciation of his critics.

'I have said it before and I will no doubt say it again,' he began, 'that I have no intention whatsoever at this point in time of challenging Miss Valerie Singleton for her job as key presenter of this quite superb children's television magazine programme. I really couldn't make myself any clearer.' He then resumed the tale of the cakes, prior to welcoming the boys and girls of Taunton High into the studio to sing a medley of seasonal verses, lanterns all aglow.

Within days of this announcement, the world learnt that Miss Valerie Singleton was indeed facing a challenge to her doughty stewardship of the programme. Mid-way through an item on how to turn an old clothes brush into an attractive and unusual Christmas tree decoration ('simply tie a piece of string around it'), Val was visibly irked to find a hand straying into shot bearing a large pair of household scissors. Snap! Within seconds, the old clothes brush had fallen to the floor, causing the Christmas tree to lose much of its lustre. A vicious trick, and though Heseltine issued strong denials that the hand was his, repeated re-runs of the film confirmed that the flamboyant initials engraved upon the signet ring were the telltale 'MH'.

Of what happened in the next few weeks, no-one can be sure. Let it suffice to say that Val mounted an effective counter-offensive and, shortly afterwards, an official announcement confirmed the replacement of Michael Heseltine with the then unknown Mr John Noakes.

The next few years must have been hard for Michael. He picked up the odd job here and there – modelling the cover of the Gorringes autumn catalogue, clad in thornproofs, trilby on head, duck-quack in hand; a stint as Captain Troy Tempest's Number Two in a short-lived stage production of *Stingray* at the Yvonne Arnaud Theatre, Guildford; the role of Sinister Country Squire ('There's something I don't quite like about him,' said Steed) in an episode of *The Avengers* – but none of these roles lent him quite the weight he needed for a full-blown career in politics.

During the mid-Sixties (dread decade!) he continued to pay his subscription to Equity, though engagements were few and far between. Leafing through back-copies of that most excellent of journals, *The Stage and Television Today*, I note with interest his repeated insertion of boxed advertisements, the majority of them thanking producers and impresarios the length and breadth of

the country for the odd week of gainful employment.
'MIKE AND BERNIE HESELTINE extend their
WARMEST THANKS for a record-breaking week at
THE REGAL WESTON-SUPER-MARE and are
DELIGHTED to announce ALL DATES STILL AVAIL-
ABLE for bookings through 1965, 1966 and 1967'
reads one such advertisement. A photograph of 'Mike
and Bernie Heseltine' replete with jocular expressions
and winning winks completes the picture. Incidentally,
historians might care to note that the aforesaid sidekick,
Bernie Heseltine, bears a striking resemblance to the
man who was to become better known as Mr Michael
Mates, MP for Hampshire East (though not, it must be
admitted, all that much better known, alas).

Closer inspection suggests that this double act consisted of a little comedy, a little juggling, and maybe
the occasional sleight of hand. One of Mike and Bernie
Heseltine's most successful 'routines' consisted of Mike
Heseltine asking Bernie how many supporters there
were in the audience. Bernie would then double the
number, add twenty, multiply by three, and report back,
all the while keeping a thoroughly straight face!

By 1966, their arch-rivals, Mike and Bernie Winters,
were beginning to make it big, with guest spots on
Saturday Night at the London Palladium, and the
Heseltines decided to call it a day, switching horses by
filling in application papers for Conservative seats in
the Home Counties at a time when such a thing was
out of fashion. Impressing selection committees with
their firm handshakes and way with words, they were
both adopted and feted amidst much applause. It now
seemed to Michael that success, for so long a stranger,
was finally beckoning.

It has been said by his contemporaries that Michael
Heseltine has had his eye on the portals of Number 10
since first he wrestled with puberty. To my mind, his
showbiz background will stand him in good stead
should ever he achieve that goal. But until that day

dawns, he would be well advised to resume contact with the Advertising Manager of *The Stage and Television Today*, methinks.

The House of Lords

EXTENDING A WARM WELCOME TO THE YOUNG
LORD MOYNIHAN

No snob I; of that there can be little doubt. I number among my close friends many who were educated outside the private system (Lord Jenkins of Hillhead, for instance, or poor old Cecil Parkinson) and even a couple who went to no school whatsoever (HM The Queen, HRH Princess Margaret). And I need hardly remind regular readers that I played an integral role in the selection of a young airline pilot called Tebbit to fight Labour in the crucial 1970 election, arguing 'Let's play 'em at their own game'.

Furthermore, I continue to support such worthy causes as my pet charity, Elocution for the Underprivileged, rejoicing in the opportunity to take slum children to the seaside, so that they can learn to assemble the deck chairs, swab out the litter, and so forth. So it is from an unassailable position of affection for the, shall we say, 'bottom drawer' that I take issue with last Sunday's cowardly attack on that most enduring of all our institutions, The House of Lords.

It goes without saying that the level of debate in the Upper House is infinitely higher than the common-or-garden brawling in the Commons. Only last Friday, I took pleasure in witnessing this delightful exchange between two Peers who, though politically poles apart, were united in decorum:

Lord Callaghan: May I in turn thank my Noble friend

for his kind words and offer him my most hearty congratulations on an excellent speech.

Lord Fawsley: In reply, may I thank my Noble friend for his kind words and offer him my most hearty congratulations on an excellent speech.

Lord Callaghan: In reply, may I thank my Noble friend for his kinds words and offer him my most hearty congratulations on an excellent speech.

Lord Fawsley: In reply, may I –

Lord Brabazon of Tara: I'm awfully sorry, my Lords, but may I, in turn, just interrupt to thank both my Noble friends for their kind words and to offer them my most hearty congratulations on their excellent speeches.

Lord Callaghan: May I accept my Noble friend's apologies with due gratitude and may I in turn thank him for his kind words and offer him my most hearty congratulations on his excellent speech . . .

How infinitely more *civilised* the Upper House reveals itself through such exchanges than its more supposedly 'democratic' (dread word!) counterpart across the way! Yet the *Independent on Sunday* (independent of *whom*, one wonders? Not Kinnock, I fear!) suggests that the very fact that we are soon to be governed by the fledgling Lord Moynihan, the ten-month son of a Filipino masseuse, is some sort of an argument against an hereditary upper chamber!

Many of Their Noble Lordships would, I believe, welcome the ministrations of the young, lightly-bronzed lad of a Filipino masseuse, happily taking whatever the boy had to offer lying down. It is, in reality, the least snobbish of institutions, its disparate membership drawn from a tremendous variety of the smarter clubs in the SW1 area, each ready to serve his country to the very best of his ability, right up until the election of a Labour government.

Few people realise the heavy burden of sheer hard

slog undertaken by the Upper Chamber. At one moment, a Peer might be hard at work on a speech applauding an opponent. Barely six months later, he will find himself drafting a suggestion to the Catering Committee on matters gastronomic. Then suddenly, before the year is out, he could be forced to lend his support on an issue of public concern close to his heart, such as the consolidation of inherited wealth or vital improvements to restrictions on rambling. Let us neither carp nor whinge, but instead warmly congratulate the new Lord Moynihan as he places his wealth of experience at the service of Their Lordship's House.

An Initiation

My many faithful readers have, I suppose, a picture of myself as the doughty scrivener whose weekly lucubrations offer them a tantalising glimpse into intellectual and political worlds from which they must otherwise feel excluded. But I have, in my day, worn other caps, among them that of the jester. My celebrated collections – among them, *Pardon My Swahili! – The Punch Book of Wallace Arnold on Abroad* (1972) and *The Unfairer Sex! – Arnold On Women* (1976) – bear testament to my skill as a humorist, and many a Lord's Taverners dinner dance has been enlivened by one of Arnold's jocular 'send-ups'. My inventions of such comical characters as Len Gunge, the Trade Unionist and Lady Featherbrain-Nonsensical, the muddle-headed female supporter of sanctions against South Africa(!) still live in the memory, and I have it on good authority that no less a personage than the Duke of Edinburgh regularly dines out on my uproarious description of almost meeting the great Len Hutton in 1961.

It was armed with such anecdotes that, in the spring of 1955, I ventured into the august offices of *The Daily Telegraph*. A mere whipper-snapper, I had been tipped off that a sense of humour would be quite an asset in one's dealings with the senior figures therein assembled. Keen as mustard to be taken on, I wandered into reception with a twinkle in my eye and a swagger in my step.

'I have an appointment with the Editor of this illustrious journal,' I announced at 10.45 am precisely.

'Down pub,' replied the receptionist. 'Say Flossie sent you.'

'Ahem,' I rejoindered, 'perhaps the Deputy Editor has taken over his duties.'

'Deputy Editor's down pub too,' replied the receptionist, looking at her watch. 'It's his turn at the darts. Tell him from me, Flossie says don't piss it down t'plughole, matey.'

Still wearing the brightest of smiles, I pushed open the door to the saloon bar, only to find my path blocked by three ruffians trading punches and splashing pint pots hither and thither. Upon enquiry, I was informed that these were the day's leader writers, getting to grips with the newspaper's line on the Maori Land-Rights Bill which faced the New Zealand Parliament at the time.

'Who you starin' at, mush?' I was asked by a figure slumped over a drinking straw poking out of the top of a bottle of Gordon's Gin. I recognised him at once as the Rev Simeon St Just, the newspaper's Religious Affairs Correspondent. 'Loved your piece on the role of Faith, Hope and Charity in the modern church last Wednesday,' I said, trusting such a compliment might appease him. 'Up your arse,' he replied, smashing a pint pot over the head of a neighbouring Salesroom Correspondent, and thrusting it in my direction.

Meanwhile a dishevelled ruffian, about whose attire there lingered the distinct aroma of urine, knelt on the floor beside me, a throaty cackle emerging from his gullet as he engaged himself in tying my shoelaces together. 'This is absurd!' I remonstrated. 'I demand to see the Editor!'

'I *am* the Editor!' replied the ruffian, and the rest of the dubious clientele began to stamp their feet in the coarsest fashion, all the while chanting, 'He *is* the Editor! He *is* the Editor!'

In order to assert my dignity, I took a step back from the braying mob, only to keel over, owing to the 'practical joke' that had been so devilishly applied to my walking shoes.

'So you're after a job, are ye, laddy?' smirked the Editor as I dusted myself down, straightening my necktie and re-puffing the spotted handkerchief in my breast pocket.

'I wish, sir, to write for a respectable family newspaper,' I declared.

'Then you've come to the right place,' replied the Editor, ejecting a gobbet of spent saliva onto the sawdust at his feet. 'If Mr Arnold wants the test, then let's give it to 'im lads!'

Even now, a full thirty-five years on, I shudder to recall the indignities to which I was then subjected. First, the Rev Simeon St Just gave me what he described as the 'Sound of Religion' test, in which I was forced to argue for a full five minutes against the use of castanets in the pulpit after first consuming a most unpleasant mixture of advocaat, vodka, Heinz tomato ketchup, cough linctus, cherry brandy and a medium-dry sherry. My trousers were then removed and treacle smeared over my 'private parts' by the then Diplomatic Correspondent while I was compelled to recite a list of ten arguments in favour of the retention of an hereditary peerage.

All, alas, was not yet over. The Editor, whom I had been forewarned was something of a stickler for etiquette, demanded that I conduct myself through a five-course white-tie dinner with Her Majesty the Queen (played by the young and then untitled Terry Worsthorne), all the while having Ind Coope Best Bitter poured over my head from a great height by the newspaper's Financial Editor, known to everyone simply as 'Arfur'.

It was while standing on one leg on the bar listing the six qualities required from an archbishop that I decided I could take no more, and an ambulance was duly summoned. A rum bunch indeed, though one might never have guessed it from their civilised and well-honed prose.

Jest in Peace, Mr Punch!

FOND MEMORIES OF A JOCULAR JOURNAL

'Might I pray silence on midships perchance that I may be permitted to ponder awhile the inestimable perils afforded the doughty – if hard-pressed! – male of the species by that most treacherous of modern contraptions, the common-or-garden vacuum cleaner?!'

The above sentence – splendidly humorous, delightfully whimsical, full of old-fashioned charm and, rarest of all in these harsh days, lacking the faintest hint of malice, was the first I ever wrote for *Punch* magazine, way back in the early Fifties. From that time on, I have been a stalwart – the backbone, some might argue – of that most chucklesome(!) of periodicals, contributing such classics of Great British humour as:

- 'If it's Wednesday it Must be Belgium: Arnold On The European Trail with the Great Unwashed' (July, 1954)
- 'Pretty Brolly! Wallace Arnold Goes Shopping for an Umbrella – and Showers the Rest of us with Laughter!' (September, 1961)
- 'Shiver Me Timbers Me Hearties – Punch All at Sea' (anthology of Nautical Humour, foreword by HRH The Duke of Edinburgh, edited by W. Arnold, 1965)
- 'Gor Blimey Guv, Oi'm 'Aving a Snooze!: Arnold Encounters the Great British Worker – and Lives to Tell this Tale!' (June, 1970)

These deliciously light-hearted pieces, and many more besides (who, for instance, can forget my long-running comic character Mr Fred Slacker, the militant Trade Unionist?) have entered the annals of British comedy, to be perused and giggled over by generations to come. But what of the mirth-filled magazine that gave them birth? The news this week that *Punch* magazine is set to close is indeed a bitter pill to swallow. In the circumstances, might one be permitted a nostalgic 'trip down memory lane' – or 'memory motorway'(!) as I once endearingly termed it (February, 1975).

After my overnight success with my fun-filled frolic on the Great British vacuum cleaner (reprinted, I am delighted to record, in *Pardon My Plug! The Punch Book of Impossible Household Contraptions!* foreword by HRH Princess Anne, edited by Libby Purves, 1983), I was invited to partake of a light-hearted luncheon at the historic Punch table by the then Editor, Mr J. Enoch Powell, later to find some measure of fame as a Member of Parliament. Having just taken over the reins of the magazine, Enoch had set about pioneering a new type of humour, which might be loosely described as removing all 'jokes', a policy the magazine has pursued to notable effect ever since.

Around that illustrious table with Enoch and myself sat, among others, HRH The Duke of Edinburgh, Miss Enid Blyton, Sir Kenneth Clark, Miss Helen Keller, General de Gaulle, Mrs Fanny Craddock and the young Paul Johnson. As you might imagine, there was laughter all the way. I trust I am giving no secrets away when I reveal that the famous *Punch* luncheon did not disperse that day until just before 2.15pm!

Ah, memories, memories . . . the occasion in the late Seventies when the then Editor, Bill Davis M. M. (Master of Mirth!), came up with the ingenious idea of getting Sheridan Morley to dress up as a daffodil for the Chelsea Flower Show . . . or when Libby Purves wrote her famous series of highly comical articles about Coping with the Kids . . . or the then Editor, Alfred Sherman, coming up with the bright idea of getting

Captain Mark Phillips to review a new book on horse trials; the Captain agreed, sent in his review, and we printed it the very next week! Who can forget the time we asked Clement Freud to test ride a Penny-Farthing?! Or the issue in which Roy Hattersley – a veritable master of the light essay – revealed his secret passion for the children's comics of yesteryear, as well as an abiding love of Shakespeare? Golden memories, one and all.

Mr Philip Larkin

You will have noted by now that the letters of my old friend and quaffing partner Philip Larkin are soon to see the light of day. A word in your ear, if I may.

The old curmudgeon was a very dear friend of mine, exchanging letters with me at least once every five or six years. 'The Librarian seeks to remind W. Arnold that his borrowing of the book(s) listed below is now overdue' reads one of my most treasured missives from Philip. 'If not returned within 7 (seven) days a statutory fine will be imposed. No further reminder will be sent'. A veritable gem, surely?

As one of the board of Faber, I was keen as mustard to see as much of his unpublished writing in print as soon as poss . . . preferably with learned introductions by yours truly! Few people knew Philip as well as I: I saw him once for a cup of coffee on Crewe station in the late Seventies, and a further three times before his death in 1985: twice in the offices of Faber and once on the dread gogglebox.

At first I was saddened to see that his will seemed to suggest a disinclination to publish any further jottings. 'I direct that all unpublished writings and diaries and texts and manuscripts in any form whether or not published at the date of my death and in my possession at the date of my death shall be destroyed unread'. Truth to tell, there was some consternation among the board that we should be forced to deprive the reading public of so many literary gems. Such was my upset, indeed, that I reached into my breast-pocket for my pipe, and took a score of deep puffs whilst contemplating our moral dilemma.

As always, the pipe did the trick. On a second, closer reading, we began to realise that this passage seemed to hint very strongly ('unpublished writings ... shall be ... read') that the poet was in fact calling for the urgent publication of all his jottings, whatever their so-called 'quality'. Between us, we literary executors and board members agreed that all letters from the Baneful Bard should be rounded up ready for publication. 'Philip would, I have no doubt, thank us for our discreet, sensitive and above all *imaginative* interpretation of his last will and testament,' I concluded, offering everyone a medium-dry sherry from the Faber decanter on their way out.

Soon, the Larkin letters were arriving by the proverbial bucketload, and sterling stuff they were too, demonstrating yet again that inestimable poet's marvellously maudlin yet perceptive humour. Soon, I was keeping a private list of some of the choicer plums:

Larkin on Seamus Heaney: 'Gombeen Man'
Larkin on Proust: 'Old Froggy'
Larkin on T. S. Eliot: 'goes on a bit'
Larkin on The Queen: 'coarse'
Larkin on Jane Austen: 'buxom wench'
Larkin on Shakespeare: 'Bearded nancy-boy'.

Delicious! Needless to say, when a Larkin letter arrived containing a witty reference to my old friend Sir Kingsley Amis, I telephoned him *tout suite* with the news. 'Marvellous stuff, Kingers!' I exclaimed, 'Larkin called you – wait for it! – "that old Bore"! Wonderful, eh?'

Oddly enough, at that very moment the line went dead. I am told that that evening saw an unparalleled rise in exterior damage to motor vehicles – broken aerials and suchlike – in the Primrose Hill area of London, but I have no doubt that, as always, dear old Kingers saw the funny side.

But discretion must sometimes be employed to save a deceased author from himself. A few months ago, just as we were assembling the final draft of the finished manuscript, a couple of late Larkin letters came in. By chance, they both made pointed reference to myself, his long-standing friend and literary mentor. In the first, he wrongly described me as 'that stupid fart, Arnold', and in the second, he referred in passing to 'a pompous twat called Wallace Arnold'.

As I say, sometimes a deceased author must be saved from himself. The ill-judged, dirty-minded and intemperate nature of those two hastily-written letters – never, incidentally, intended for publication – stood seriously to damage Larkin's reputation as a writer and poet. I thus had no hesitation in seeing to their destruction, as Philip would have wished. As I have long maintained, the wishes of an author must be paramount, particularly when he also happens to be a very dear friend.

LIGHTNING O'ERHEAD

The Sixties: Decade Of Discontent

Wallace Arnold: Welcome to my Wireless. Welcome to my World.

The Fab Four. The Satire Boom. 'Letting It All Hang Out'. The Mini Skirt. Dread words indeed, and all taken from that most dread of all decades – the 1960s. Pardon my shudders!

In January, 1960, the Sixties began, in the same callous spirit as they meant to go on, with the announcement that the Queen's only sister, Princess Margaret-Rose, was now engaged to a 'photographer' called Jones. I suppose we can all remember exactly where we were when first we heard that ghastly news. I myself, by now a much-loved household name in the world of broadcasting, was the lynch-pin of a team of distinguished celebrities competing in a new series for the wireless called *Just One Minute Thirty-Five Seconds*, later to become better known in its revised second series as *Just a Minute*, and presented, at that time, by the young Quintin Hogg:

*

(Crackly radio noises)

Quintin Hogg: Hands on buzzers, gentlemen, please. Wallace Arnold, may I ask you to speak for 'Just One Minute Thirty-Five Seconds' on the following subject, Sniffle Music . . . commencing . . . now!

Wallace Arnold: I'm awfully sorry, but are you sure you don't mean 'Skiffle Music'?

(BUZZ)

Derek Nimmo: Hesitation!

Quintin Hogg: Granted!

Wallace Arnold: *(laughing aggressively)* Look here, I'm awfully sorry, but there's no such thing as 'Sniffle Music'.

Quintin Hogg: There's no question about it, the letters on this card read, from left to right, S – N – I – F *(pause)* I'm sorry. I have just been asked that this edition of *Just One Minute Thirty-Five Seconds* make way for an important news announcement from our Founder.

Lord Reith: This is Lord Reith speaking. It is with the very deepest regret that we have learnt news of the engagement of Her Royal Highness Princess Margaret to a photographer called Jones. Our thoughts remain with the Royal Family at this most distressing of times.

('God Save the Queen')

Quintin Hogg: Sniffle. Skiffle. Tiffle. Piffle. Who the jolly heck cares any more? Wallace Arnold, speak for however long you jolly well want on 'The Beginning of the End' starting . . . now!

*

Wallace Arnold: The year of 1961 saw a brief lull before the much-trumpeted arrival of 'The Permissive Society' in 1962. The record books confirm that little happened in 1961 apart from the death of a Swiss Psychoanalyst with a name most normal people regarded as completely unpronounceable, a topic about which I was to wax most lyrical when I made my debut on a new programme for the Home Service, billed as 'forty minutes of lively and topical conversation'. I am talking, of course, of the immortal *Stop the Week*, since, ahem, disbanded. So let's sit back and enjoy an extract from that, introduced then, as always, by Uncle Bob Robinson:

*

Robert Robinson: Incidentally, as we are on the subject – or not as the case may be! – I wonder if anyone else heard tell of the death last weekend of someone who rejoiced to describe himself – heaven forfend! – as an Eminent Swiss Psychoanalyst, if you please!

(Chuckles of fellow panellists)

His name – and I kid you not! – was – and I have it here on a card in front of me! – Carl JUNG. That's J – U – N – G. Hardly a Home Counties name, I would aver. *(more chuckles)* 'Have you met the Jungs of East Molesey?' As an introduction that somehow doesn't ring quite true. *(more chuckles)* But how, I ask myself, should one *pronounce* the blessed name? Is it really JUNG to rhyme with BUNG and TONGUE? Wallace Arnold, you look to me the type of fellow who knows a thing or two about Eminent Swiss Psychoanalysts!

(More chuckles)

Wallace Arnold: Thank you, Bob – though I'm not sure that's a compliment!

Robert Robinson: It was, I assure you most heartily, intended as such!

Wallace Arnold: Well, Bob, I rather favour JOONGE. **(chuckles)** or – better still – JUNGE to rhyme with LUNGE!

(Chuckles)

Robert Robinson: I think, sir, you may well have a

point! Ann Lesley, what has your benificent eye
alighted upon this week, perchance?

Ann Lesley: Well, Bob, this week, I've been out and
about testing five different types of new nail varnish
– a case, if you will, of THE LADY VARNISHES!

(Chuckles and fade)

*

Wallace Arnold: *(small nostalgic chuckle)* There we
were pulling the proverbial leg of the 'Psychology'
boffins in a delightfully light-hearted fashion. But
within a year we were being asked to move on. A
new type of 'humour' was on its way. Yes, the dread
Satire Boom had arrived.

Of course, Satire was nothing new. A sense of
humour is not, nor has it ever been – thank goodness!
– the sole prerogative of the Hard Left. For six agreeable years, I had rejoiced in the title of Motoring
Editor of Punch, that most jocular of journals, and I
was widely-known as the creator of such immortal
comic classics as *If It's Wednesday, It Must Be
Bognor!* My humorous wireless series on the perils
and pitfalls of motoring, *Pardon My Hooter!*, had
become something of a firm favourite with the house-
wives. Who can forget, for instance, my classic
comedy 'routine', *A Typical Working-Class Family
Goes Motoring*, co-written, incidentally, with my old
quaffing partner Kingsley Amis, and showing something of his sure hand with everyday dialogue. Needless to say, it starred yours truly as the immortal
'Dad':

*

(Studio audience laughter)

Dad: *(with terrible working-class accent)* Ay-Up,
Mum, there's summat t'matter wiv t'vee-hic-cul!

(Explosion followed by uproarious laughter from studio audience)

Mum: Oo-er. What mikes you think thet, Dad?

(Further explosion. More laughter)

Dad: Let's av a look. I'm now lookin' under the bonnet. Oh, no! Our bread and dripping sarnies have gone all black, Mum!

Mum: Why's that, Dad?

Dad: I put them in the petrol tank for safe-keeping!

(Explosion, uproarious laughter, jaunty music, applause)

Wallace Arnold: Priceless, surely?! But the smart alecs of the Satire Boom weren't content with rib-tickling comic observation: oh, no, it was the downfall of British society that *they* were after. And pretty soon they got it. *Private Eye. The Establishment Club. Beyond the Fringe. That Was The Week That Was.* In 1963, these cold-hearted satirists paved the way for the Profumo Scandal, the Philby Affair, The Great Train Robbery and the downfall of the Macmillan Government, all in the same tragic year. And the repercussions are still with us today, in work-shy hippies, the dirty-fingernail brigade, marauding joy-riders and sex for one and all. And I still bear the scars. Four years ago, in 1989, Dr Anthony Clare invited me to take my place *In the Psychiatrist's Chair*. In that most memorable and moving pro-gramme, listeners tuned in in amazement as their wireless companion for so many decades shed his few remaining layers of skin to reveal a deep inner *hurt*:

*

Dr Anthony Clare: Tell me about it.

Wallace Arnold: I'd rather n–.

Dr Anthony Clare: Please.

Wallace Arnold: *(big sigh)* It's not something I – *big sigh).* It's – hard, very . . . hard. *(Sound of muffled sobs)*

Dr Anthony Clare: Come on, poppet. Deep breath. All better now. Big hug. Good boy.

Wallace Arnold: I'm sorry, I –.

Dr Anthony Clare: Not at all.

Wallace Arnold: I feel . . . such a fool. I don't know . . . what came over me.

Dr Anthony Clare: Big blow.

(Sound of Wallace Arnold blowing his nose)

Dr Anthony Clare: All better. That's a brave fellow. So . . . if I can return . . . you were obviously severely traumatised by the downfall of Macmillan and the prospect of seven years of Labour government?

*

Wallace Arnold: Harrowing listening. *(Takes deep breath)* In the mid-Sixties, everything went topsy-turvy. It was the era of The Beatles and The Rolling Stones, of long hair, hard drugs, 'josh' sticks, jeans, 'polo' necks and psychedelia *(pronounced 'sitchedelia').* Princess Margaret was seen to attend the world premiere of the Beatles film, *A Hard Day's Night.* Royalty were acting like 'pop' stars, and 'pop' stars were acting like Royalty. At that fateful premiere, leading commentators found it impossible to distinguish between the Princess and Mr Ringo Starr, for both were wearing the same suit and had attended the same hair salon prior to their official meeting. Only when Princess Margaret failed to keep the beat on the opening bars of 'I Want To Hold Your Hand' did the truth emerge.

It was around this time that the dread new phrase, 'Classless Society'(!) began to poke its nose out from under the proverbial floorboards. Edward Heath became the first grammar-school boy to be elected leader of the Tory Party. Each of The Beatles was awarded the MBE. Princess Anne went up with other members of the audience of the 'hippy musical' *Hair* and danced on stage in a purple trouser suit. The Prince of Wales appeared onstage in a dustbin for the Cambridge University *Footlights* revue. An American walked on the Moon. Dread Era indeed! Things would never be the same again, and to some the phrase 'Swinging London' would remain the most disagreeable of all conundrums:

*

Wallace Arnold: . . . and if the plucky England squad under the admirable Bobby Moore can manage to win the World Cup in such sterling fashion, I see no reason whatsoever why we as a country should not honour their magnificent achievement by reintroducing Capital Punishment – *and not a moment too soon!*

(Roars of approval, applause)

David Jacobs: Thank you, Wallace Arnold. And can we have the next questioner, please?

The young Cecil Parkinson: Cecil Parkinson. I'm a gentlemen's hairstylist aged 36 from Romford.

David Jacobs: And your question, please, Mr Parkinson?

Cecil Parkinson: What does the panel think is meant by 'Swinging London'?

David Jacobs: Cecil Parkinson, a gentlemen's hairstylist from Romford, wants to know what the panel think is meant by the term 'Swinging London'. The Right Honourable Enoch Powell?

Enoch Powell: It is a question the meaning of which seems to me illogical and consequently incomprehensible. For London to swing it would require suspension on an apparatus designed for that purpose, positioned many tens of miles up in the air, with all the attendant girders, pulleys, ropes, platforms and chains. Has this happened? I think not. Therefore the phrase 'Swinging London' is without meaning, by which I mean 'meaning' in the true meaning of the word 'meaning', by which I mean a meaning of 'meaning' meaning . . .

(Fades)

Wallace Arnold: By 1969, the Sixties, as they had come to be known, had got quite out of hand. The Royal Guild of Haberdashers and Dental Assistants had commissioned an up-and-coming painter by the name of Francis Bacon to paint their Honorary Patron, Queen Elizabeth the Queen Mother, only to find, at the unveiling, that Her Majesty had been portrayed naked but for a sheep's carcass on her head, screaming blue murder at a triangle in the top right corner. Everywhere, ancient institutions were under threat, nowhere more so than the Home Service, now renamed 'Radio Four' in the jargon of the time.

It was in the July of that year that I took over *Down Your Way* when its regular presenter, Franklin Engelmann, took to his hols. It was to be broadcast from the beautiful village of Bardfield on the Isle of Wight, but we had reckoned without the monstrous influence of that dread decade:

*

(Down Your Way *theme music: Birds twittering*)

Wallace Arnold: Good Afternoon everybody, and this is your old friend Wallace Arnold inviting you to join me 'Down Your Way, in the lovely village of Bardfield, where I'm sure we'll meet many a marvellous old character. Here's one now, for instance. Good afternoon, sir, and your name is – ?

Bob Dylan: Dylan. Bob Dylan.

Wallace Arnold: Dylan Bob Dylan! Marvellous old

country name for you there. And I'd guess you've seem some changes in your time, Dylan Bob Dylan!?

Bob Dylan: *(singing)* 'The times they are a' changin'.'

Wallace Arnold: Quite. But let's hope all these changes are what I would call 'in keeping'. I imagine quite a few of your agreeable homegrown crafts still manage to delight both visitor and local alike?

Bob Dylan: *(singing)* 'And don't criticise what you can't understand.'

Wallace Arnold: And now we move to a really charming old character dressed in all the colours of the rainbow, lovely bright blues and mauves. And your name is?

Janis Joplin: Janis Joplin, dickhead.

Wallace Arnold: Janis Joplin Dickhead. Now that's a name to conjure with!

*

Wallace Arnold: Convention had been thrown to the winds. The dirty-fingernail brigade was in the ascendant. Loutishness, poor grammar, mini skirts and general sloppiness abounded. But worse was to follow. As midnight struck on December 31st, 1969, the Sixties were to usher in that most dread of decades, the Seventies, an era I shall be explaining in greater detail next week. Until then, this is Wallace Arnold saying, 'Welcome to my Wireless. Welcome to my World'.

Mr John Major

THE HISTORY OF A WARM FRIENDSHIP

I must confess myself a little surprised that Mr Edward Pearce has not seen fit to include me in his new biography of Mr John Major for I have, of course, been on intimate terms with our new Prime Minister for close on twenty years. Might I come to the aid of future historians and fill in those gaps which Pearce, perhaps from jealousy, perhaps out of misguided deference, chose to leave unfilled?

I first met John way back in 1969, when he served me a bag of 6″ screws from behind the counter of a leading ironmongers in the Brentford area. If it was indeed him – and I have no reason to suppose that it was not, for this assistant had a deferential air and very pronounced spectacles – then our conversation went like this:

W.A.: A bag of 6″ screws, please.

J.M.: Certainly, sir. That'll be thirty-five new pence, please.

W.A.: *(handing over correct change)* Thank you.

J.M.: Who's next please?

It was another ten years before I renewed our brief acquaintance. He had just been elected to the House of Commons, and on his third day as an MP he was delighted to be invited to a small cocktail party where 'new boys' could mix freely with what one might call the 'grandees' of the party such as W. Arnold esq. I was expounding on, as I remember, the Common Market (dread words!) when, out of the corner of one eye, I saw him approach. I immediately thrust out an empty glass in his general direction.

'A touch more fizz for me, please, waiter,' I exclaimed, by way of greeting. 'B-b-but I am the new MP for Huntingdon' he explained, fidgeting with the middle button of his jacket.

'*Excusez-moi* – they're spreading such a wide net these days that it's deuce hard to keep up!' I explained, seeking to put him at his ease. 'What's your name, laddy?'

'Major,' he replied, jigging from foot to foot.

'Major by name,' I muttered to my old quaffing-partner Mr Julian Critchley, 'but Corporal by nature!'

John couldn't help but overhear this good-natured quip, and he was, as I remember, the first to join in the merriment, looking down with a straight face at his somewhat over-shined shoes in, I believe, silent laughter. And from that moment on, our friendship never looked back.

For the next eight years we did not, I seem to remember, exchange so much as a word, though mutual friends now tell me that he used to nod and smile enthusiastically in my direction if ever we passed in a Westminster corridor. It was on his elevation to Chief Secretary to the Treasury in 1987 that I became aware that our friendship was of a more enduring type than I had previously suspected. 'My dear John,' I wrote. 'Heartiest congrats on your appointment! Delighted that Margaret took my advice! Must have lunch soon! Yrs ever, Wallace. P.S. Love to the wife (if any).' And, do you know, I still keep his reply to this day. 'The Chief Secretary read your recent communication with great interest,' it reads. 'He appreciates all comment from members of the public and has asked me to convey his thanks.'

Mr Robert Maxwell (i)

I PAY TOUCHING TRIBUTE TO THE LARGER-THAN-LIFE ENTREPRENEUR

Those wise enough to have purchased Mr Joe Haines's authoritative biography of Robert Maxwell, *Maxwell* (Macdonald, 1988) will recall the lavish display of photographs every hundred pages or so.

'Robert Maxwell discussing world affairs with Henry Kissinger in Tokyo' reads the caption to one, 'Maxwell shares a laugh with President Moi in Nairobi' another. Further on: 'A break for laughter with President Zhikov of Bulgaria', 'An informal presentation to the Princess of Wales', 'Cordial greetings to Deng Xiaoping', 'A private word with Wallace Arnold', 'An informal round of clock golf with President Ceaucescu of Romania', and 'Trading wit and wisdom with Leonid Brezhnev'.

Needless to say, my links with the late Bob Maxwell have led to a very busy week. We struck up a close friendship back in 1981, a handsome cheque from the National Bank and Safe Deposit Facility of Lichtenstein finding its way into my Coutts bank account after I had effected a breakfast meeting between him and my old friend and client Princess Michael of Kent. A couple of years later, impressed by my contacts in what one might call High Society, he placed the guest list and general arrangements for his now legendary sixtieth birthday party in my hands.

The queue of distinguished guests I assembled outside Headington Hall that night was indeed impressive. From David Frost to Jim Callaghan, from Sir Robin Day to Harold Wilson: all had come to sup at Bob's table. 'Welcome! Welcome!' Bob would bellow good-heartedly at each guest as he entered, 'And who are you?' The guest would then state his full name – 'President Mitterand of France', 'The Imperial Duke Vladimir', 'The Rt Hon Mr and Mrs Neil Kinnock' – to a uniformed security guard before being ushered into a neighbouring room for a full body search. With all arms or offensive weapons stowed safely away for collection on departure, the guest would be presented with a delightful hand-picked commemorative gift – an embossed leather toilet case (for the gentlemen) or a fully automatic five-speed battery or mains operated hairdryer (for the ladies) – before being required to pass into a large downstairs room to contribute a glowing tribute to their host for inclusion in a presentation *Festschrift* under exam conditions.

Once the tribute had been judged up to the standard set by the external examiners, the guest would be permitted to exit through the far door. Here he would be handed a large card with a small portion of a capital letter on one side and on the other, a tiny area from a photograph of Bob's face – a few square inches of chin, perhaps, or half a nasal hair. There followed three-quarters of an hour of rigorous practice for the synchronised card twirling that was to be the highlight of the evening, one side of the triumphal assemblage showing Bob's beaming visage, the other proclaiming 'WE LOVE YOU, BOB!'

I need hardly add that the birthday party was a huge success, each of the guests coming away, as had been agreed by contract, with a party bag containing: *a)* a cheque for £1500; *b)* a whole cooked lobster; *c)* a signed photograph of Robert Maxwell, MC; *d)* a half bottle of Remy Martin High Quality Cognac; *e)* a novelty hat plus humorous motto; *f)* a Boots voucher value £25 redeemable at all Boots stores nationwide. 'You've done me proud, Wallace,' Bob said as the last guest was shooed away by the trained dog-handler. 'And to think that those wonderful people – all pre-eminent in their fields, I might add – so adore me!'

And so to the sorry events of the past week. Many of those present at that party found themselves badgered by the media (dread word!) to pay public tribute to their old friend and patron. Of course, their first action was to seek my advice. No man of the world would wish to compromise his position with too eloquent a display of affection for the compromised corpse, yet to say nothing at all might seem standoffish, perhaps even shadey. My advice? Choose any two from the following list – unique, larger than life, ebullient, truly larger than life, dynamic, remarkable, tremendous appetite, enthusiastic, colourful, very much larger than life – deliver your choice through your solicitor to the Press Association, issue no further statements. Sifting through the week's tributes, I note with approval that most of them saw fit to follow my directive.

Mr Robert Maxwell (ii)

I GIVE THE OLD ROGUE A PIECE OF MY MIND

Amid much unseemly conjecture, might I at least be granted this opportunity to explain my role as a former director of Mirror Group Newspapers whose resignation yesterday has come as such an undeserved blow to so many employees?

Upon accepting Mr Robert Maxwell's invitation to join the board in the late spring of 1986, I made it crystal clear that he must be prepared for some doughty questioning from my quarter. I was not prepared, I told him, merely to sit back and let him run roughshod. The same went for my fellow directors Lord Havers of Haverhill, Lord Donoghue of Doncaster and Lord Williams of Willesden. We pondered our position long and hard, eventually setting out our case to Maxwell in a strong memo ('We the undersigned vow to resign immediately at the merest suggestion of impropriety'). I still have this memo about my person – we decided against giving it to him, feeling it might undermine our positions – and it remains available to all who wish to study it.

Earlier this year, I had cause to cross-question Maxwell over luncheon on a one-to-one basis about rumours surrounding the Mirror Group Pension Fund. As is my practice, I took the bull by the horns. 'Bob,' I said, raising one eyebrow. He looked back at me. I could tell from his expression – at once alarmed yet respectful – that he knew very well what I meant. Judging it right to let the matter rest there, I then said,

'Pass the gravy, please,' and joined him in a starter of medium-rare Chateaubriand, followed by leg of lamb, fully shorn, with rice pud and Black Forest Gateau to follow. By the end of our agreeable luncheon, I knew full well that he had taken my warning to heart, for he never mentioned it again.

Of course, I had long held my suspicions, but to raise aggressive 'questions' would, I knew perfectly well, be the coward's way out. Instead, I continued to sit on the board, ever alert for that moment when I could get to the bottom of things and present my grave forebodings to the Chairman – quite regardless of personal consequence – at a full boardroom meeting.

With great patience, I bided my time. When the opportunity arose, I leapt like the proverbial tiger. No-one, but no-one, was now going to tell Arnold to hold his fire. 'In my considered view,' I boomed to a packed boardroom, 'it is high time the complex manoeuvres and questionable practices of the Chairman were subjected to the fullest investigation.' I then turned to his empty chair. 'He may have died a month ago,' I continued – a mite fearful, but by now convinced that I was doing the right thing – 'but his actions continue to haunt us.' This was a full two days ago. Others might have urged caution, but that is not the stuff, alas, of which Arnolds are made.

Having established my credentials as something of a whistle-blower, might I move on to tackle the most important question of all. How do we continue to safeguard the integrity and quality of that great newspaper, *The Daily Mirror*? It is worth reminding ourselves that it has built a worldwide reputation for serious, no-frills reportage of the national and international issues of the day, written in a manner accessible to the ordinary working 'bloke'. One has only to think of that great newspaper's recent hard-hitting campaigns on behalf of the elderly ('Ger'em Off, Gramps! – Horny Grans in Sex Romps', Aug, 1990) and for closer union with

Europe ('Maastrips! – Dutch Caps Come Out as Major Flies In!', Nov, 1991) and of the space The Mirror Group has devoted to issues that many would prefer to dodge ('Loony Perv Eats OAP, Leaves Bones', Jan, 1989) to realise the unfathomable loss to the nation were it to be changed in any way.

The calibre of its staff, too, is second to none, and that is why *The Daily Mirror* has been awarded the prestigious 'Press Society Award for Best Weather and Road Condition Reports 1973 (Runner Up)' as well as our very own *Heart of Gold* medal from TV's Esther Rantzen for our moving report on the plight of Britain's wildlife ('Pet Hamster Dies in Car Swerve Drama', March, 1991). Let us build on this glorious past by putting the events of the last few weeks behind us and, perhaps even more importantly, let us signal our confidence to the world by reinstating our directors without another second's delay.

Monsieur Mayle, mon Ami

This week past, I have been enjoying a well-earned rest *au Provence* with my old *ami* and quaffing partner, *Monsieur Peter Mayle* of that parish.

As my three works for the kitchen – *Arnold on Anchovies* (1971), *Wallace Arnold's 500 Uses for Pork Luncheon Meat* (1983), and my 1990 Glenfiddich award-winning *The Age-Old Art of Napkin-Folding* all attest, I am an avid and immensely knowledgeable lover of food. My sojourn with Peter has, I am glad to say, reinvigorated the old taste buds sufficiently to goad me into offering you, over the next fifteen weeks, a vivid pen-portrait of some of the magnificent repasts we enjoyed in delightful little out-of-the-way *bistros* and *brasseries* in our beloved *Provence*.

First stop was the front parlour of the indomitable *Madame Bonbon*, who is reputed to serve the best Pigeonhead Soufflé in the whole of the *Luberon*. Like the old pro she is, Madame insists on biting the heads off the young pigeons herself. She then uses the frantic flap of their taut young wings to wind-dry their heads, which are then placed prettily amid an ocean of fresh thyme and aragula, ripe plum tomatoes and a *soupçon* of Madame's own *saliva* before being ground with traditional pestle and mortar and mixed with the yolks of four free-range eggs before being placed in a piping hot oven for just three minutes. Result: *magnifique*!

'You will find that *Madame Bonbon*,' announced Peter as we drove at brisk pace through the winding lanes of the *Luberon*, 'is something of a character.' How right he was! As I soon learnt, she makes great play of simply loathing *les Anglais*, and *Monsieur Mayle* in particular, slapping him in the face with jocular abandon, verbally abusing his *chère maman* with her marvellous peasant tongue, taking great pains to bar all doors against our impending entry.

'Tremendous fighter, *Madame Bonbon*,' chuckled Peter as a bucketful of cow-dung descended upon him from the dizzy heights of an upper window of that agreeable old *Provençale* farmhouse.

After delightful *badinage* had been exchanged, we managed to gain entry to *Madame*'s pantry by means of an unbolted catflap. I rather think that *Madame* must have been impressed by our tenacity, for her mood seemed to soften as she mixed an *Apéritif de la Maison* for us, a local speciality, she proudly declared, consisting of equal portions *kir*, *armagnac* and caustic soda.

Over a sumptuous repast of coxcomb wrapped in ox tongue with a deliciously light hare and blackcurrant sauce, washed down with wonderfully rough *vin de table* from a neighbouring well, we proceeded to inform *Madame* of the culinary developments 'back home'.

The ignorance of the French is really quite something. Sorry to say, after repeated cross-questioning it emerged that the poor woman had never even heard of Mrs Elizabeth David! Stifling my astonishment, I informed her, in the most civil manner possible, that Mrs David had put French provincial cooking firmly on the map, and that she was an idol to many millions of Englishmen both at home and abroad. It was even said, I added, that many miracles had been performed in Mrs David's name, and that once, after she had passed through an untended meadow in Wales, literally hundreds of small pots of *bouillabaisse* had sprung up in her wake.

We sat in that spartan farmhouse room, never happier, regaling the doughty *Madame* for hours on end with tale upon tale of Mrs David's good works before a knock on the door signalled the entrance of the local *gendarme*, firmly but politely asking us to leave the premises within thirty seconds.

I hope that this word-picture of life *au Provence* has served to awaken this column's many devotees to some of the good things in life, and that it has stimulated those taste buds for my forthcoming fifteen-part cut-out-and-keep cookery series, *A Teaspoon of Lard and a Glass of Sanatogen* (© Arnold Promotions), for which embossed leather binders are already available. So, until *la semaine prochaine*, from Peter M. and my own good self – *BON APPETIT!*

The most Natural Person in the World

LILIBET, OF COURSE!

My friends – of whom I sometimes feel I am blessed with more than I can cope! – have spent the past week praising my appearance on the BBC's documentary programme about Her Majesty the Queen. I was featured, of course, prominent among those who had earned their spurs. If by any chance you missed me, I was the fellow to the left of my old friend and quiffing partner Sir Peregrine Worsthorne, and to the right of my one-time associate but hardly what one might call a friend, Sir Peter Clowes (least said, soonest mended!).

Though it was the first time I have ever been knighted, I have known Lilibet on and off for a good many years, proffering her advice and/or comfort as and when required, but otherwise simply soaking up the sheer fun of her gracious presence. It is this marvellous sense of humour and, as my old friend Sir Roy Strong might put it, *joie de vivre*, that was so delightfully exhibited throughout the BBC's quite excellent programme: a side of Lilibet for too long hidden from the general public, but much coveted by those she holds dear.

Might I offer one or two further examples of Her Majesty the Queen's ready wit, culled from my own collection? They are largely drawn, I might add, from my forthcoming volume, *The Faber Book of Respectful Royal Anecdotes*, edited by Sir Wallace Arnold (320pp, £17.95).

The year is 1961, the venue Windsor Castle. At the time, I was the young Court Correspondent of *The*

Daily Telegraph, invited to an intimate royal cocktail
party with the more salubrious of my fellow scriveners.
The Queen Mother, never more radiant, was there, her
laughter twinkling like a rare pearl in the soft azure
sky, her smile positively medicinal in its effect on one
and all. Beside her stood Her Majesty, speaking to a
small circle of courtiers and admirers in that natural,
unaffected way of hers, wisely employing her tongue
and lips. Never had I seen her more carefree, never more
resplendent, her skin unblemished, her wit unparalleled.

'May I humbly suggest, ma'am, that we are indeed
blessed and most deeply gratified to be here tonight in
your most gracious presence,' intoned my fellow
wordsmith Godfrey Talbot, in an attempt to, as it were,
'break the ice'.

'And might I add,' I chipped in, 'that those of us
lucky enough to have been granted invitations to this
most enchanting of evenings are doubly delighted, never
having seen Your Majesty looking so regal, nor so . . .
so . . . so – '

'Natural,' chipped in Godfrey, and we all agreed.

'Yes indeed – *natural!*' quoth I.

At this point Her Majesty issued one of those priceless, perfectly-timed observations that have long been
her forte. She bided her time, waiting till I had finished
speaking, and then said:

'Thank you very much.'

Needless to say, we all *peeled* with laughter, Godfrey
even leading a discreet round of applause, each one of
us making a mental note of the witticism so that we
could repeat it, verbatim, to future generations. Of
course, a literal transcription does scant justice to the
brilliance of her timing, but to those of us there present,
it was a revelation of that remarkable lady's great gift
for comedy.

My other anecdote comes from that much-maligned
former Prime Minister, Lord Callaghan of Cardiff. It
was 1966, and Jim was at a select dinner party at

the Palace with his Cabinet colleagues Dick Crossman, Anthony Crosland and Harold (later Lord) Wilson. At the end of dinner, Callaghan, a socialist to his bones, made an informal speech thanking Her Majesty for 'your great kindness and munificence, your gracious bonhomie and your supreme poise'.

There was a hushed silence, and then The Queen, sheer, unadulterated wit alive in her eyes, quipped:

'Thank you very much.'

Needless to say, the company positively *roared* with laughter. Once again, she had made their day. Further affectionate anecdotes most gratefully received, incidentally.

NIGHT FALLS

The Seventies: Decade Of Disaster

Wallace Arnold: Welcome to my Wireless. Welcome to my World. Watergate. Gary Glitter. Ambassador Jay. The Poulson Affair. The Ayatollah. John and Yoko. The Winter of Discontent. Streaking. The Third Man. The Fourth Man. The Fifth Man. The *Umpteenth* Man.

The 1970s were a shabby affair, the grim harvest we reaped for the excesses of the dread 1960s.

The Seventies were characterised by a pervasive melancholy, by scandal after scandal, strike after strike, vulgarity after vulgarity. Britain had lost not only its Empire but also its get-up-and-go. Anything that *could* get worse *did* get worse. Jimmy Carter. Deep Throat. John Stonehouse. Decimalisation. Britain's entry into the EEC. The three day week. Saturday Night Fever.

Grim days indeed. Yet it had all started on such a note of optimism. Listen to this extract, for instance, from the first 1970 edition of *Start the Week*, then in its infancy, and presented, with characteristic aplomb, by yours truly, Wallace Arnold:

*

(Radio pips)

Announcer: And now, with the time just gone 9.00, we invite you to usher in a fresh decade of topical discussion with the first *Start the Week* of the 1970s, presented, as ever, by Wallace Arnold.

Wallace Arnold: Welcome to my Wireless. Welcome to my World. And a very warm Welcome to the new Decade. My guests today include five men for whom the Seventies hold out a wide variety of exciting possibilities. So a very good morning to the renowned community architect who has done so much to breathe life back into our inner cities – Mr John Poulson . . .

John Poulson: Good morning.

Wallace Arnold: . . . Lord Lambton, widely tipped for a Ministerial post in the event of a Conservative victory at the polls . . .

Lord Lambton: Good morning.

Wallace Arnold: and from the rapidly-expanding Liberal benches in the House of Commons, a gentleman who can always be relied upon to add a touch of levity if the times grow dark. I'm talking of course of Mr Jeremy Thorpe . . .

Jeremy Thorpe: A very good morning to you.

Wallace Arnold: . . . and from the less worldly groves of academe, the highly respected art historian, Professor Sir Anthony Blunt . . .

Sir Anthony Blunt: Good morning.

Wallace Arnold: . . . and finally, the high-flying Labour MP – widely tipped as a future leader of his party, and at the moment rejoicing in the title of Postmaster General, no less – Mr John Stonehouse.

John Stonehouse: Good morning, Wallace.

Wallace Arnold: So, gentlemen – should one enter this decade of the Seventies in a spirit of hope, a spirit of optimism?

All at the same time: Oh, yes, undoubtedly
Very much so
Absolutely
. . . Ray of sunshine . . .
Tremendous optimism
Rather!

*

Wallace Arnold: The decade began, in characteristically muddling fashion, with the introduction of the New Money. Instead of good, old-fashioned pounds, shillings and pence – not to mention that most agreeable of denominations, the trusty guinea! – we were subjected to that most insubstantial of phenomena – THE NEW PEE. The cost to one's deeper feelings of patriotism and conservation were only to emerge nearly twenty years later when I spoke of the traumas of the early Seventies with Dr Anthony Clare on my celebrated 1989 debut *In the Psychiatrist's Chair*:

*

Wallace Arnold: *(deep breaths, splutters)*
Dr Anthony Clare: It obviously upset you very much.
Wallace Arnold: That's ... yes, yes, that's right. Very ... much *(deep breath, small sob)*. I'm sorry.
Dr Anthony Clare: Was it the new ten pence piece, do you think, or the hexagonal fifty pence piece, or was it the accumulation of all these new coins?
Wallace Arnold: I ... don't ... know ... Oh, god ...
Dr Anthony Clare: Come on. Big blow.

(Sound of Wallace Arnold blowing nose)

Dr Anthony Clare: All better now. All better.

*

Wallace Arnold: It was not only within the realm of the coinage that the limits of human endurance were being put to the test. The year 1970 had seen the premiere of the lewd show, *Oh Calcutta* followed shortly afterwards by Miss (Msss!) Germaine Greer's *The Female Uncle*. But 1973 saw a brief ray of hope. I am talking, of course, of the premiere of *Jesus Christ Su-u-perstar*, a life-affirming musical by two very

bright young public schoolboys – Tim Rice and
Andrew Lloyd Webber.

In that very same year, the Home Service had
launched its new arts magazine programme – still
going strong – yes, *Kaleidoscope*. As one of the first
presenters of this new show, I was called upon to
present a special edition devoted to this tremendously
exciting new musical. In conversation with leading
churchmen and the bright young composers themselves, I learnt that it was a show full of deeper
spiritual resonance, a beacon of joy in difficult times.
In those days, as now, I should remind you that it
was – and still is! – the custom in *Kaleidoscope* to
insert the word 'extraordinary' – or variations thereof
– into the programme once every thirty seconds or
so. This is for purely technical reasons, allowing the
duty engineer to test the sound quality:

*

Voice Singing: Jesus Christ. Su-u-perstar.
You must be exhausted.
Have you come far?
Jesus Christ. Su-u-perstar
Did you come by foot as
They haven't invented the car?

Wallace Arnold: The extraordinarily evocative title
song from the new West End rock opera, *Jesus Christ
Su-u-perstar*. Good evening, this is Wallace Arnold
saying Welcome to my World, Welcome to my Wireless, and welcome to this special edition of our new
arts magazine programme, *Kaleidoscope*. Before I ask
my studio guests about this remarkable effort by two
young public school boys, let's hear just one more
snatch. Here, in one of the most moving moments of
the first act, Jesus Christ Su-u-perstar greets Judas
Iscariot:

Voice Singing: 'Iscariot! Iscariot!
Your first name is Judas

I don't think it's Harriet!
Iscariot! Iscariot!
You travel by donkey
In preference to chariot!

Wallace Arnold: Extraordinarily palatable. Reverend David Jenkins, you are a leading man of the cloth – what do you make of this rock-musical? Extraordinary?

David Jenkins: Extraordinary in every way. It breathes new life into the tired Christian message in a way that I for one find tremendously *relevant* and above all . . .

Wallace Arnold: Extraordinary?

David Jenkins: Yes – extraordinary.

Wallace Arnold: Yes, I too found it quite extraordinary.

David Jenkins: Almost in a way extraordinarily extraordinary.

Wallace Arnold: Indeed, so extraordinarily extraordinary that I'm almost tempted to call it . . .

David Jenkins: . . . Extraordinary?

Wallace Arnold: Quite.

David Jenkins: Quite extraordinary.

*

Wallace Arnold: For a short time, *Jesus Christ Su-u-perstar* allowed us all to forget that we were still in the early days of what was to be – along with the Fifties, the Sixties and the Eighties – one of the gloomiest of all postwar decades. Before you could mention the proverbial cutting implement, scandal was piled onto sadness, misery onto horror. The dread year 1972 saw Britain joining the EEC, the Poulson and Watergate affairs, my old friend and quaffing partner Lord Lambton being caught with his alas-not-so-proverbial trousers down, the Three Day Week . . . and the marriage of Her Royal Highness Princess Anne to Captain Mark Phillips. Sorry days indeed.

And then came news of the death of Nancy Mitford, most prominent of those immortal Mitford sisters (Mecca the errant Muslim, Decca the recording artiste, Recca the highly-strung terrorist, Becca the tennis champion, Necca the nymphomaniac and Pecca the tragic anorexic). It had been Nancy, of course, who had invented those delicious terms 'U' and 'Non U' to define correct language and behaviour in what one might call 'society'. In those dark days of the 1970s, with the world disintegrating all about us, we seemed to need her guidance more than ever, as I made clear, time and time again, on *Any Questions*:

*

Conservative MP: And let me add this, for all those who would seek to mollycoddle the young miscreant. Capital punishment never did me any harm. Oh, no. A good strong slap to my backside or a clip around the ear from the village bobby, a sharp whack from a cane or, failing that, a gym-shoe, a bare hand coming down jolly hard on the bare buttocks, a twelve-inch ruler applied with great force by a uniformed officer, a chain, lavishly spiked . . .

(Cheers and ferocious applause)

David Jacobs: And could we move on to the next question please.

Sidney Vicious: *(obviously reading)* Sidney Vicious aged sixteen from South London. In these world-weary times, does the panel think that good manners have fallen by the wayside and, more importantly, can anything be done about it?

David Jacobs: Young Sidney Vicious wants to know whether, in these world-weary times, you think that good manners have fallen by the wayside and, if so, whether anything can be done about it. Wallace?

Wallace Arnold: Might I kick off by saying that if only more of the youth of today showed the common courtesy and sheer good manners evinced by young Sidney Vicious, this great country of ours would have little to worry about! It can only bode well for the future. Keep it up, Sidney!

(Cheers and applause)

And so to the question: yes, I regret to say that I *do* think good manners, etiquette and decent grammar have fallen by the wayside. Only the other day I was parading along Regent Street when I chanced upon a scruffy old woman wearing plastic bags over her feet rather than sensible shoes, a hat made of soggy old newspapers – and I won't say which newspapers! – and clothes which looked as if, to say the least, they could do with a jolly good wash. 'Ere, Guv,' she said to me, and for a split second I thought she was Spanish, 'Ere, Guv – gissa penny for a cuppa, love.' Perhaps she meant to say, 'Excuse me, sir, but I was wondering if you would most generously contribute any small change you might have towards the cost of a cup of tea, thanks awfully'. If she had done so, I might indeed have dipped into my pocket. But then why didn't she say it? Something must be done!

(Applause and cheers)

*

Wallace Arnold: By the mid-Seventies, the dread affairs were piling up thick and fast. The Watergate Affair. The Slag Heap Affair. The Lucan Affair. The Stonehouse Affair. The Slater-Walker Affair. The Thorpe Affair. But a ray of sunshine can light up even the stormiest weather, as the immortal *Desert Island Discs* set out to prove when they invited yours truly to be their thirteen hundred and twenty-third guest in June, 1977:

*

(Dying strains of 'My Way')

Roy Plomley: Frank Sinatra singing 'My Way'. Wallace
Arnold, music obviously means a lot to you.

Wallace Arnold: An immeasurable amount, Roy. I love
classical music with a passion. Opera. Very moving.
The Third Programme. Indispensable. Let's hope they
never change it. Glyndebourne. Highly civilised.
Music without any words. Even better than music
with. I love the lot, the older the better.

Roy Plomley: Any particular favourite composer?

Wallace Arnold: Ummm . . . I love them all really, just
as long as they're classical! Batch . . .

Roy Plomley: . . . You have a batch of favourite composers?

Wallace Arnold: No. *Batch*. Johann Sebastian Batch.
He's a great favourite.

Roy Plomley: Any special piece of music by Johann
Sebastian . . . by er . . . by that particular
composer . . . ?

Wallace Arnold: By Batch?

Roy Plomley: Yes . . . by er B – by er B – by er –
Wallace Arnold, how do you think you would fend
on this Desert Island? Are you a practical man?

*

Wallace Arnold: Impressive indeed. Incidentally, as an
historical footnote, I pride myself on being the only
guest in the history of *Desert Island Discs* to have
chosen 'My Way' by Frank Sinatra twice – as both
my second and my seventh choice of disc! Splendid!
But one swallow, as the poet once said, doth not
make a summer, and the Seventies were due to end
upon the sourest of notes. In 1976, the Sex Pistols
disported themselves in unruly manner across our
television sets, and by 1979 The Shah of Iran had
been forced to make way for the Ayatollah Khomeini
while in Britain the rubbish piled up on the streets.
All was gloom and despair. Virtually all of those
guests I had entertained on that first *Start the Week*

of the decade had found themselves in the dock, in despair or in disgrace. But then a woman came onto the scene who changed all that. A woman, who, back in 1978, had not been correctly identified by any one of the four contestants on *Brain of Britain*:

*

Robert Robinson: Your penultimate question, gentlemen. Who is the only female member of the Shadow Cabinet in the present Opposition, Mr Pritchard?

Mr Pritchard: Francis Pym?

Robert Robinson: No. Mr Gossett?

Mr Gossett: Sir Christopher Soames?

Robert Robinson: Nice try, but no. Mr Assington?

Mr Assington: Willie Whitelaw?

Robert Robinson: No. Mr Simpkins?

Mr Simpkins: Geoffrey Rippon?

Robert Robinson: Brave stab, Mr Simpkins, but the answer is in fact a Mrs Margaret Thatcher, T-H-A-T-C-H-E-R. Well, you learn something new each day. And finally, something rather easier – what is the correct Latin title of the East African lizard better known to most of us as a Laskovi Artirobulus?

*

Wallace Arnold: Yet the next decade was to become known as the Thatcher Decade, though friends tell me that for regular listeners to the wireless it might also be judged The Arnold Decade. That decade was, of course, the Eighties, an era I shall be explaining in full next week. Until then, this is Wallace Arnold saying 'Welcome to my Wireless. Welcome to my World'.

The Old Devil

HIS BEST SINCE *LUCKY JIM!*

'The Old Devil(!) has done it again. For those – and there are still a few of us about – who relish a damn good (not to mention *in*decent) belly-laugh, the new novel by Amis *père* is a veritable treasure trove.'

You probably read Arnold on Amis in *The Telegraph* last week. I described his new novel, *The Russian Thingy* (Hutchinson, £17.95) as 'easily his best since *Lucky Jim*. Amis has never been so funny – or so true'. This has, of course, been my standard Amis review since the early Seventies (dread decade!), updated only once, in 1987, when I added the marvellously intimate sentence, 'Those of us who have spent many a riotous evening supping the odd jar – or three! – with Kingers will delight to see the Old Devil back on top form once more'.

To be frank, I am reliably informed that his new one is not up to much, so I daresay I'll be leaving it for the all-too proverbial 'rainy day'. Nevertheless, it is always a delight to give Kingers a bit of a leg-up, a sentiment shared by all those who trooped off to his 70th birthday celebrations at The Savoy (or 'The Saveloy' as we must learn to call it now that old Forte has his fingers in the pie!).

Needless to say, the Old Devil was in cracking form, sounding off over the preprandial lemon squash (I jest) about everything from toast ('disgusting bready stuff') to lawns ('why must they always be so bloody *green*?'), not forgetting that most hardy of all his perennials –

the so-called 'fairer sex' ('Why don't they wear jackets and ties like the rest of us? I'll tell you why. Can't be bloody bothered! Too bloody *effeminate*').

All his old friends had turned up – save those he had maligned in his deliciously waspish *Memoirs* – and as the three of us moved through to the dining room Kingers sounded off about toothbrushes ('Ever tried shaving with one? Of course not. No bloody good at getting the stubble off, that's why') and the sun ('Always bloody *shining*'). He then delivered a short 70th birthday speech. I trust that the Old Devil(!) will forgive me if I reprint some of the choicest extracts for the benefit of those mere mortals whose invitations to The Saveloy may have gone sadly astray!

He kicked off with a delightful range of money-saving tips, the product of seventy years of keeping his nose to the ground and his back to the wall. Might I reprint just three of these veritable gems?

(1) Always save your old corks. They make excellent ear-plugs for when the ladies begin getting touchy.
(2) Never waste money on flowers. They are offensively bright and they pong.
(3) If you've agreed to take someone out to dinner, take care to book the restaurant table for just one. 'Bloody waiters. Can't even get a bloody booking right,' you can then complain from your single setting as you bid a cheery toodle-oo to your pal, who must now learn to sponge elsewhere.

The Old Devil closed his speech by offering us a selection of his priceless imitations, a showcase, incidentally, for his marvellous ear for the nuances of everyday speech. 'Blow me darn wiv a fevver,' he said, imitating a cockney news vendor. 'That'll be foive bob, mister!' He then proceeded to impersonate – quite hilariously! – an Indian waiter, declaring 'Blow me darn wiv a fevver! Dat'll be foive bob, mister!', and ended, to great hoots of laughter from all and sundry, with a consummate impersonation of a typical Somerset farmer ('Arrh! Blow me darn wiv a fevver! That'll be foive bob, mister!').

Needless to say, the rest of us were in fits as the minestrone plus bread roll arrived. Alas, this estimable starter did not meet with the approval of the Master. 'What's this?' he barked, his eyes popping out on stalks, his face growing purple with rage. 'Someone's bloody sneezed into the broth!'

Priceless! But it is too easy to forget, among all these heart-warming fol-de-rols, that Amis is also a novelist at the very height of his powers. He is as capable of turning his hand to a novel about, say, the awful women who surround a poor chap who doesn't know whether he's coming or going, as he is to a novel about a poor chap who doesn't know whether he's coming or going, and who finds himself surrounded by awful women. I now eagerly await his next novel – easily his best since *Lucky Jim*, forsooth.

The Old School Tie

To answer your unspoken question, I shall, of course, be venturing down to Eton come Tuesday next, there to partake of the fireworks and fizz in honour of 550 illustrious years. That estimable institution deserves the encouragement and support of all old boys, and I will be foremost among those who will be donning their furks and scugs in order to bully the rip into a Strawberry Mess as the Monarch comes over the bum freezer.

Looking back on my days at Eton, I find my memories go into a sort of dreamy haze for, to be perfectly honest, I did not attend Eton College as a pupil as such, but instead spent a very full five years at celebrated Basters Hall near Reigate, which was, of course, something of a sister school, and was rightly regarded by Eton as a key rival. Many of the Basters' traditions, though stretching back only seventeen years at the time, were based upon the very best that Eton had to offer, and so I feel, in a curious way, that I enjoyed all the advantages of an Eton education with few of the drawbacks.

Basters Hall was founded in 1931 by a select group of gentlemen from the Basting profession. Its origins are still celebrated, both in the school shield, which depicts a couple of basting spoons pouring best fat over a sizzling turkey, and in its Basting Day tradition, where pupils line up along the school wall to be Basted by the Head Man, and Matron stands by with swathes of cotton wool, ready to bathe any heat wound.

Celebrated Old Basterds include, from the armed

services, Major P. Simpson and many others; from the world of the arts, Tony S. Sharpe, who crops up in a great many episodes of *Softly, Softly* and is soon to be seen in the *Taggart* series on television; many captains of industry, including the brains behind Chumley's Sausages and, of course, from the world of politics, a great feather in the school's cap, the present Home Secretary, Mr David Waddington.

David and I were contemporaries, and we would always be out, come rain or shine, to cheer on the school team with rousing cries of 'Baste up, the Basters! Baste up! Baste up! Baste up!' Looking back, the Arnold/Waddington era probably constituted the golden years of Basters Hall, a time to rival that inter-war period at Eton when Acton would Pop his Fly with Connolly while Burgess Tugged his Jordan in the Sock with Orwell.

Our distinctive school uniform – dark grey suit and sober tie – cut something of a dash on our occasional visits to Reigate, and set us apart from hoi polloi, breeding in us a sense of our own distinction. Like Eton, Basters fostered self-confidence, poise and, above all, a sense of classical learning in her sons. To this day, David Waddington is able to recite most of his twelve times table without recourse to notes, and I still have a good many tunes from the very best of Gilbert and Sullivan under my belt. At odd times of the day, I find myself humming The Basting Song ('Baste that Bird, Almighty/Baste him till he's brown'), and you may well catch me whistling it, a tear in my eye, come Tuesday.

Dr David Owen

IN CELEBRATION OF A FRANK AND REALISTIC
AUTOBIOGRAPHY

It is an open secret in and along the corridors of power
that I 'helped' (*nota bene* the inverted commas!) Dr
Owen with his previous volumes of autobiography,
Declaring the Time (1974), *Timing the Declaration*
(1981) and *A Time to Recline* (1985), as well as his
slim volume of occasional verse, *A Rhyme to Decline*.
I was also, I can now admit, the principal architect
behind four mould-breaking SDP discussion documents,
A Future for the Present (1983), *Forward with the Past*
(1984), *Towards Tomorrow* (1985) and *Tomorrow
Today: The Present in Our Future* (1986). Towards the
end of his (my!) introduction to the present volume, the
Doctor is good enough to acknowledge 'my close friend
and colleague Wallace Arnold for his tremendous assist-
ance in policy formulation and overall content, and for
being a shoulder to cry on when times got rough'. Sweet
words from a very dear friend.

Perhaps this calls for a word or two of explanation.
Though a lifelong Tory through birth, breeding, instinct
and intellect, I had welcomed Dr Owen's frank and
realistic approach to the central issues of the day. 'Let
us be frank and realistic about this,' I remember hearing
him say on breakfast television shortly after the formation of the Gang of Four, 'the situation in which this
country finds itself calls for an increasingly frank and
realistic approach.' Brave words indeed, and I knew at
once that here was a politician who was able to look

beyond the confines of narrow party issues towards a vision both realistic and frank.

Within a matter of minutes, I had contacted the good Doctor's office to offer my skilled advice on matters of presentation and deportment. Having previously advised Keith Joseph, Mark Thatcher and Robert Maxwell, I was instantly welcomed to Dr Owen's entourage in order to conduct a series of lessons in Personal Grooming. As Dr Owen was a politician with what is known in the trade as 'bottom', out went his single-vent jacket, to be replaced by a double-venter, allowing more room for his fuller-figured posterior to 'breathe', as it were. Next, I contacted a leading hairdresser, Roberto of Mayfair, and had him run the Doctor up a small hairpiece designed in the shape of a flapping 'quiff', which, attached to a discreet electronic timepiece, would fall down upon his brow once every 45 seconds. The Doctor would then emit a 'frank and realistic' while employing his right hand to push the quiff in a devil-may-care fashion back into place. This, I need hardly add, greatly aided his standing as a man of moral vision, never one to let a stray strand stand in the way of a train of thought.

It goes without saying that the politicians Owen attracted were of the very highest calibre. I believed then, as I believe now, that Mrs Rosie Barnes would have made a first-class Chancellor of the Exchequer, while Mr John Cartwright's easy-going charisma would have earned him plaudits on the world stage as one of our most effective Foreign Secretaries. As it is, within the year Rosie will be resuming her position behind the cashier's till in Sainsbury's while John will be catching up on all the latest trends in computer programming.

Such is fate, yet how well I remember the great spirit of hope that coursed through the room while I was preparing Dr Owen for his state-of-the-nation address to the SDP Conference in Bournemouth back in 1986. The party was at an all-time high, with Dr Owen's private pollsters placing him ten points above Mr Kinnock, five points above Mrs Thatcher and only a marginal three points below Mr David Penhaligon, who was to meet his end in an untimely car accident just four months later. Dr Owen's hair, now under my direct supervision, had won many accolades too – among them Plymouth and Devonport Male Creation of the Year (Medical Section) – and his double-vented jacket was also beginning to show through in the polls.

'David, my dear,' I said, as he entered that rehearsal room armed with his speech. 'Simply can't wait for the address. Might one be allowed to inquire of its subject matter?'

'It's on the need for frankness. And not just frankness, but a fair measure of – '

'Realism?' I suggested.

'Exactly. Frankness and realism. It's what my public expects of me, and what they'll expect of my government next year, the year after and, frankly, for the rest of the century. By the way, I was thinking of moving Rosie from the Exchequer to Home Secretary, with poor old Steel perhaps having a little corner-desk at Transport. What d'ye think, Wallace, realistically?'

Heady days indeed, but the great swing to the Social Democrats was, alas, never to be. Rather than winning an overall majority of 320 seats, as Dr Owen had estimated at his most frank and realistic, the Social Democrats polled a comparatively disappointing three. Happily, the Doctor himself appeared not to be bothered by this result. Ever since, he has carried on his Prime Ministerial duties as usual, issuing frank warnings to Saddam Hussein, urging greater realism upon company bosses, doing his utmost to keep productivity in line with inflation and personally supervising the country's long haul to greater prosperity. Recently, it has been hinted that Owen has invited the influential Mr John Major MP to lend his backing to the SDP, in return for the promise of a seat in the next Owenite government.

Will Major be tempted to accept? On a close reading of this book, it would be hard for anyone not to believe that David is, indeed, the greatest peacetime Prime Minister we have ever had.

Mr Christopher Patten

A DOUGHTY CAMPAIGNER!

It is always gratifying when one of one's youthful proto-gées makes his mark; never more so than in the case of Mr Chris Patten, of whom an Arnoldian pen-portrait is, I regret, long o'erdue.

I first bumped into Christopher (as he then was!) back in the summer of '64. At the time, I was writer-in-residence at Conservative Central Office, burning the midnight oil composing letters, pamphlets, leaked memos and secret documents concerning some of what one might call our less savoury opponents in the forth-coming General Election. My sheer hard work was paying dividends, and the list still reads pretty impress-ively to this day:

- 'Jim Callaghan a Nazi Spy? Leaked Memo "Still Unproven"' (*Daily Express*, August 4th, 1964)
- 'Barbara Castle in Nude Blancmange Dance Drama Rumour' (*Daily Mail*, August 7th, 1964)
- 'Healey Sex Change? Insiders Suggest Denis to Become Denise "Within Weeks"' (*Evening Standard*, August 12th, 1964)
- 'George Brown Sacrifices Lamb, Molests Pensioner, Pledges to Raise Taxes, Drinks Too Much and Leaks Top Secrets to Russia: Could This Happen Here?' (*Sunday Express*, August 22nd, 1964)
- 'Crossman Denies Eating Child with Redcurrant Jelly' (*Daily Mail*, August 27th, 1964)
- 'Sir Alec in Line For Guildford and District Tailors

and Cutters Association Best-Dressed Man Award: Personal Cleanliness Highly Praised' (*Evening Standard*, August 29th, 1964)

But success breeds its own pressures, and work was beginning to 'get on top of me' (dread phrase!) when the fresh-faced young figure of Christopher P. came a-knocking at my door. My initial impression was one of extraordinary sensitivity to the feelings of others, combined with a very real feeling for the underdog. 'We must target the poor and underprivileged' he maintained, the youthful idealism of the Young Conservative glowing in his eyes. 'For instance, how about: "Poor and Underprivileged in Russian Spy Ring: Prosecutions Pending"?'

I offered him the job of my chief assistant there and then, and before the day was out we had placed another of his creations – 'Society's Underdogs in Moscow Sex Pervert Secret Memo: Kathy Kirby "Not Involved" ' – in the *Sunday Express*, where it merited a splash headline. This, the ever-accurate Arnold instincts informed me, was a young chap who was, to employ the modish jargon current at the time, 'Going Places – And Fast'.

It is impossible to understand Chris without first appreciating the depth of his Catholicism. Over the past few weeks, for instance, he has been going to Confession two, three, or even four times a day, sometimes after each major telephone call to a Sunday newspaper, always emerging refreshed and invigorated, ready to set the political agenda in time for the *Six O'Clock News*.

As the Election approaches, I have urged him again and again to concentrate on the positive side of Conservative policies and personalities rather than stooping to denigrate our opponents. I am glad to say Chris is with me all the way. We have, we both agree, first-class candidates and first-class policies, and we will be riding on these assets in next month's national poster campaign – 'John Major: Never a Party Leader To Have An Affair With His Secretary'.

Poor People Make Good Cushions

AND OTHER ARNOLDIAN PAMPHLETS FOR THE
CENTRE FOR POLICY STUDIES

Ever since the early Seventies, when I injected some
much-needed intellectual rigour into Conservative
thought with my pamphlet *Poor People Make Good
Cushions* (35p), urging the revival of the stuffed fabric
industry in industrial Lancashire, the top dogs at Central Office have listened to the word of Arnold with
ears keenly cocked.

I suspect future historians will judge my heyday at
Smith Square to have been the Parkinson era of 1981–3.
Ever since our first meeting in, if I remember rightly, a
basement club for executives in the Shepherd Market
area circa 1974, Cecil and I have, quite simply, clicked.
Even at that first meeting, he had been eager to seek
my advice about how to get on in the Party we both so
loved. Well do I remember taking him to one side and
advising him in hushed tones that centre partings were
somewhat frowned upon by the higher *echelons*, adding
that he might also think of jettisoning his rolled gold
identity bracelets and silver neck 'pendant'. Needless to
say, he followed this advice, subsequently rising to the
dizzy heights of Chairmanship of the Conservative
Party.

Fortunately for the nation, Cecil never forgot that he
owed it all to Arnold, and he was delighted to entertain
all my initiatives for boosting the Party. It was I, for
instance, who engineered the higher media profile for
Mark Thatcher in the early Eighties, realising that the

Great British Public would at once take this loveable, devil-may-care young lad to its heart. I am also to be thanked for the rise of the young Norman Lamont, whom I discovered when he was still chief assistant at the Vidal Sassoon salon in Upper Brook Street, with special responsibility for blow-dries and perms; but that, as they say, is another story.

In the summer of '81, the intellectual wing of the Party – that is to say Sir Keith Joseph, Lady Olga Maitland, ex-Jazz saxophonist Alfie Sherman, Sir John Junor, Geoffrey Dickens MP and myself – decided to form the Centre for Policy Studies, a veritable hothouse of schemes and ideas to keep the Thatcher revolution on its proverbial toes for the coming decade.

Our first meeting got off to a flying start. 'Super to be a member of the Tink Thank,' said Geoffrey Dickens.

'Think Tank,' I muttered, politely.

'Let's not split hairs,' he replied. 'What I say is, let's all think the thinkable.'

'Even better,' said Lady Olga, 'let's unthink the unthinkable.'

Ever the diplomatist, Alfie Sherman tactfully drew the best from both policy statements, and thus our stated aim, 'To think the unthinkable' was born. Vigorous new initiatives were to follow, with pamphlets galore. I rather think that it was my own trenchant tract, *Towards the Privatisation of Secretarial Services* which set the trend for Ministers above a certain level exchanging their wives for their secretaries, thus greatly reducing all-round administrative and entertainment costs while setting an example for the rest of the country to follow. I also played a large part in maintaining a consistent line in the Party's attitude to Europe with my three influential pamphlets *Europe: Seizing the Challenge* (1981), *Europe: Untangling the Web* (1983) and *Europe: The Guilty Men* (1988), in the last of which I placed the blame for our fatal liaison with Europe firmly on the terylene-suited shoulders of Mr Edward Heath (dread name!). I am delighted to announce that *Europe: Seizing the Challenge* is shortly to be re-issued (CPS £5.95).

With the next election drawing nigh I have been roped in once more to high-level talks in Smith Square. I trust I am giving no secrets away when I reveal that my old friend and quaffing partner Sir Nicholas Fairbairn will shortly be assuming a high-profile role in the arena of the party's public relations, and we are indeed fortunate in having persuaded Mr Mark Thatcher to oversee our fundraising accounts. With these two at the helm, might one who has his finger on the pulse now earnestly advise friend Kinnock to look to his – albeit proverbial! – laurels?

Saddam at the Garrick

PLUS REPERCUSSIONS

Though hardly as steeped in the rich, thoroughly British air of a Geoffrey, a Roderick or even, perchance, a Wallace, the name of Saddam Hussein seemed, at the time, more than acceptable to the goodly burghers of the Garrick Club.

I am talking now of the mid-Sixties (dread decade!) when the traditional gentlemen's clubs of London were considered by the young and ill-shaven insufficiently 'with-it' ('With *what*, precisely?' I would declare in my richly stentorian tones over a leg of finest mutton, causing, needless to say, peals of mirth from my fellow guests – but I digress!).

Nowadays, The Garrick is filled to the brim with the very greatest characters in the land – among them Mr Terry Worsthorne of *The Sunday Telegraph*, Mr Reginald Varney of *On The Buses* and several leading lights from *The Onedin Line* – but in that forlorn era it was a mere shell in which ghosts of the past seemed to hover in melancholy. By the fireplace, Mr Michael Miles might buttonhole one for a quick round of the Yes and No game before din-dins, and occasionally one would catch a glimpse of Mr Arthur Askey rehearsing his 'Buzzy Bee' routine *sotto voce* on the landing but, by and large, the 'joint' no longer 'jumped'.

Never one to miss an opportunity, Saddam, at the time something of a big noise on the staff of Burke's Peerage, sought my aid in securing membership. Impressed by his robust handshake, pleasant blazers and rich fund of Gielgud anecdotes, the Committee elected him forthwith, honouring him further with the post of Entertainments Secretary.

Alas, it was soon to emerge that Saddam's instincts were far from being those of the natural clubman. This became evident at a Royal Variety Club dinner in honour of the three most famous Beverley Sisters, Dobs, Dibs and Dabs Beverley, with their youngest sister, Antonia Beverley – later to become known as the historian Antonia Fraser – in attendance, together with a galaxy of stars from stage and screen, among them Sir Alfred Sherman. It was to be a night of warm-hearted reminiscence and impromptu rendition presided over by the honorary Gary – the term by which club members are known – HRH The Duke of Edinburgh.

It fell to Saddam to organise the various 'skits', dance sequences and folderols that were to accompany the speeches. Alas, members took it in bad odour when – shortly after an uproarious speech by the irrepressible Mr Terry Scott – who should march onto the floor but the Massed Bands of the Iraqi Fifth Airborne Division, trumpeting a little-known and frankly not catchy tune in praise of Mohammed. When the exercise in Armed Combat which followed resulted in severe injury to the Club Secretary, some members decided to signal their disapproval by refusing a liqueur with their cigars.

Having lost his position at Burke's after dropping all non-Iraqis from inclusion, leaving but a single entrant (it seems that Lord Wyatt of Weevil originally hailed from one of the better parts of Baghdad), Saddam resigned his membership and went home. A sorry business, and one with repercussions that have since become all too evident.

Lord Snooty

PRONOUNCED SN'OY

Stunned. Shell-shocked. And deeply upset. These are the only words that spring to mind when I am asked by sympathisers how I have been affected by the overnight decision to axe 'Lord Snooty and his Pals' from the *Beano* periodical.

I am told that Lord Snooty is moving comics to become Saleroom Correspondent for *The Spectator*, but this is hardly the same: for the past fifty-four years Snooty and his mixed bunch of pals have been entertaining us with their splendid antics, flying the flag for a smarter, more shipshape Britain. A solo spot for Snooty in a down-market weekly with a, frankly, less educated type of reader simply will not wash.

Lord Snooty (correctly pronounced Sn'oy) first came onto the scene in the late Thirties. Some claim he was a pseudonym for Quintin Hogg (later Lord Hailsham), others that his lofty manner and resolute quiff make him a 'dead-ringer' – whatever that might be! – for Sir Peregrine Worsthorne, whose weekly adventures have been the mainstay of *The Sunday Telegraph* comic section for these past fifty years.

But Snooty needs no imitators; he has always been very much his own man, as anyone who has witnessed his numerous appearances in the House of Lords will attest. He has long maintained a particular interest in countryside and heritage matters; he will be remembered, for instance, for his resolute attack on 'ramblers' (dread word!) when the question of new footpaths was discussed three years ago, and he is a doughty champion of bloodsports, in particular the marvellously traditional festival of rabbit-squashing that takes place in the Cotswolds on the first Sunday in February each year. My old friend and quaffing partner Sir Nicholas Fairbairn is a beneficiary of Snooty's prowess at this excellent sport, being the proud owner of a three piece suit made entirely from rabbit ears.

The current editor of the *Beano*, a Mr Euan Kerr – widely tipped, I hear, as the next Editor of *The Times* – has claimed of Snooty that 'Our readership can't relate to him . . . His top hat and Eton collar must baffle today's kids. At the time he was created in 1938, it was a more divided society. His axing is very much a part of our new classless society'. What weasel words from Kerr! Perhaps in today's more 'Kerr-ing' society(!), 'kids' must be protected from the horrors of sheer good manners, cleanliness and common decency, but for the life of me I cannot see why.

I would hazard a guess that the loathly Kerr had a hand in the other great disaster of the week, namely the decision to foreclose that most readable of periodicals, *The Victor*. Delights galore awaited the reader who was prepared to give *The Victor* a little of his time and effort. Who can forget its star-turn, the plucky Cockney athlete, Alf Tupper, The Tough of the Track?

An historical footnote: my sources tell me that Tupper was modelled on the young Norman St John Stevas, now Lord St John of Fawnsley, who came to prominence as a first-class amateur sprinter in the early Fifties, much given to expressions such as 'Bloomin' Ada' and 'Lead me to the free grub, mate, I ain't 'alf starvin' '. This fruity language was testament to his experience in the welding trade. Norman has, I need hardly add, refined such expressions over the course of an impressive political career, though once in a while the occasional 'lorluvaduck' can be heard to slip through his net, and some have argued that his impressive six-volume edition of the *Complete Works of Walter Bagehot* was marred by Norman's tendency in his scholarly introduction to refer to Bagehot as 'a really brainy geezer'.

Nor should the educational aspect of The Victor be under-rated by the so-called 'experts' (experts at *what*, may one ask?) Over the years, the 'It's a Wacky World!' column has taught me everything I know. 'In Spain, 12,000 people sat down to eat a mile-long sausage. It took 150 cooks eight hours to cook it and it weighed 3,300lb' (June 16th, 1987). Fascinating! Perhaps our sister newspaper, *The Independent* (dread word!) should take a leaf from *The Victor*'s book. Does anybody really want to know exactly when Mr Bottomley placed his bun in Mrs Bottomley's oven? Not, methinks, when Alf Tupper has another race to run!

Sorrow is my Middle Name

STEPHEN MILLICENT SORROW PERSEPHONE
TENNANT

One is so often assailed by the ponderous lives of the
unashamedly low-born(!) that it makes a welcome
change to read of my old friend and quiffing-partner,
Stephen Tennant, whose biography has received such a
stiff press from those whose shoulders are, I regret to
say, a mite chipped.

Might I be allowed to add a few memories of my
own? I will never forget my first meeting with the great
man. Dressed from top to toe as a budgerigar, he would
sit chirruping for days on end upon a specially-con-
structed perch opposite a swinging mirror, answering
only to the name of Billy, restricting himself to a diet
composed largely of nuts. It should be remembered that
we are now talking of a time before posing as a budgie
became commonplace, many years, for instance, before
the advent of Sir Roy Strong.

The next time I met Stephen he was suffering from
one of those periodic bouts of severe depression that
were to beset him throughout his life. 'Sorrow is my
middle name,' he announced in his languid drawl.
'Stephen Millicent Sorrow Persephone Tennant.' He
had been unable to lift a paintbrush for a full five years,
complaining that the splash of green paint on its tip
made it far too heavy to hold and a potential hazard
to his sensitive back, and this too made him bitterly
unhappy. Even his dressing-up now went through a
lacklustre period; he was surprised and not a little hurt
when, after he had gone to the trouble of placing a

grape pip and a banana skin on his head, his friends still failed to mistake him for Carmen Miranda.

His critics have ascribed laziness to Stephen, but this is far from the truth. He worked for twenty years polishing the first sentence of his long-promised novel, only to meet with dreadful disappointment when a close friend pointed out that it contained a number of grammatical inaccuracies, being composed entirely of adverbs. 'But my novel is to consist of nothing BUT adverbs!' responded Stephen. 'Nouns are so coarse, adjectives so common, verbs so inexorably vulgar – and as for conjunctions – *well*!'

The professional life did not agree with him. For a time, he toyed with entering the Armed Services, but the Wrens refused him a commission, and he steadfastly maintained that khaki was not really *him*, putting paid to a career on land.

Like so many rich men with fine houses and well-stocked cellars, he was the type of person for whom I had a tremendous amount of time, and many of his aphorisms were tinged with wisdom and, yes, a good deal of common sense. 'Never – *but never* – tie a pink ribbon upon a lizard. The little devil will soon wriggle out of it!' I remember him insisting over a crème de menthe in early '63, and I have followed his advice, with no little success, to this very day. 'Remember, my dear, one can do whatever one wants with one's eyelashes,' he told me in the autumn of '57 over a pink *curacao*, 'but they are *perfectly useless* for turning the pages of even the most slender of books.' Of course, in these egalitarian (dread word!) times, such a charmed life will have its critics, but more's the pity, says I, more's the pity.

STORMS AHEAD

The Eighties: Decade Of Dashed Dreams

Wallace Arnold: This is Wallace Arnold saying, 'Welcome to my Wireless. Welcome to my World'.

Hard to believe, but you have been listening to that catchphrase of mine on your wireless for four decades now. And the most recent of those decades was, of course, the 1980s.

In the Fifties, everyone was working-class and rebellious; in the Sixties, freedom went to our heads, and it all ended in tears; and in the Seventies we all paid the fearful price, suffering a three-day week, decimalisation and streaking.

Thank goodness, then, that the Eighties will be remembered as the decade that heralded the return of common sense. And throughout that delicious decade, my voice, the voice of Wallace Arnold, was your wireless companion; the voice, I have heard it said, of sunshine on even the darkest days. My friends tell me that I brought to the new decade a refreshing sense of informality – and that I was one of the few members of the BBC who could speak to leading statesmen and politicians as both friend and equal:

*

(Radio pips)

Wallace Arnold: Hello, this is the *World at One* on October 15th, 1980, with Wallace Arnold inviting you to join me for forty-five minutes of news, views and comment on this Wednesday lunchtime, the day Mr James Callaghan formally announced his resignation as leader of the Labour Party. And he is with me in the studio now. Mr Callaghan – Jim! – what are your thoughts as you leave the leadership of the Labour Party?

James Callaghan: Let's be frank about this, shall we? I honestly can't pretend that I don't have any regrets, but I think I leave my party in an excellent position for the future, with a strong measure of support from the country as a whole, and that gives me a great deal to be proud of.

Wallace Arnold: Nice to get back to the old farm, I should think, after having to deal with all those awful union types for so long!?

James Callaghan: Well, I wouldn't put it precisely like th –

Wallace Arnold: You'll much prefer it in the House of Lords, anyway – awfully comfy and infinitely more civilised! May I recommend the Chateau Branaire Ducru '61? Do you know the Duke of Carlisle?

James Callaghan: I can't say I –

Wallace Arnold: Oh, but you *must*. He'd be delighted to show you the ropes. Just tell him who you are, and that you're a friend of mine. Better not let on you're Labour though! Mind you, he'd never guess.

James Callaghan: Might I make just one or two small points at this juncture? First, my belief in the establishment of a Social Contract with our colleagues in the –

Wallace Arnold: Super. And now on to the rest of the news. There has been a major pile-up on the M4 outside Reading. What on earth would they be wanting to do in Reading, that's what I'd like to know! Joking apart, fifteen people have been rushed to hospital, where doctors say . . .

(Fades)

*

Wallace Arnold: My post on the *World at One* soon came to a close – they were really after someone a little less authoritative, shall we say, more 'the awful little man in the street'. Nevertheless, my 'dulcet tones'(!) continued to dominate the Home Service throughout the 1980s and beyond.

I was still, for instance, the irrepressible mainstay of *Stop the Week*, ever ready to deliver firm – and often lighthearted! – views on such vexed questions as when one should wear a bowler hat or how to perform the perfect rhumba. Given the call, I was even on standby to apply a goodly dose of much-needed humour to that most dread of issues, the Miners' Strike:

*

Robert Robinson: Forgive me, but I can't for the life of me stop myself thinking of it in a curious way as 'The Miner's Trike', pleasing image! *(laughter from studio guests)* conjuring up the delicious word picture of your charming old miner, sporting cloth cap and string vest, appearing at the picket line – incidentally, why 'picket' and not 'pocket' line? – *(more laughter)* on his doughty three wheeler! *(more laughter)* Wallace?

Wallace Arnold: Or indeed – forgive me, Bob – the 'My Nose Stripe!' *(slight laughter)*

Robert Robinson: Spelt?

Wallace Arnold: Let me see, that would be M-Y new word N-O-S-E new word S-T-R-I-P-E – 'my nose stripe' – referring perhaps to a stripe, or strip, of sticky plaster placed over one's hooter after some burly 'yoof'(!) has applied his fist to said conk! My Nose Stripe! *(slighter laughter)*

Robert Robinson: *(stiffly)* Let us move swiftly on. Ann,

I believe you have strong thoughts about the demise of the penny chew?

*

Wallace Arnold: And so to 1982. The Year of The Falklands. The Royal Navy was there. The British Army was there. The Royal Air Force was there. And Wallace Arnold was there, sending vivid word-pictures back for the Home Service, managing to convey all the naked excitement and fear of life on the Front Line:

*

(Sound of heavy gunfire, torpedoes, running, etc)

Wallace Arnold: *(shouting through the uproar)* I counted them all out, and blow me if I didn't completely forget to count them all back. *(explosion)* It's been a long, hard day with only one or two lives lost, five or so I think. What's that? *(Muffled consultation through sound of gunfire)* Yes, that's it, one hundred and twelve lives lost, still, could be worse, and you'll be glad to hear *(machine gun fire)* I'm holding up well, and have been congratulated more than once by senior officers on my choice of waterproofs, as well as showing great personal courage under the most trying of conditions. *(Aeroplane noise)* That's an Argy aeroplane overhead now, you can probably hear it. I'm shaking my fist at it. 'Away with you, Pedro! And that goes for you too, Gonzalez!' *(At this point, all the background war noises stop, and there is complete silence. W. A. appears taken aback by the silence)* Ah. That's shown him.

(There follows a succession of sound effects: a door opening, then birds chirruping, horses galloping, then heavy traffic, church bells, farmyard noises etc.

Through it all, W. A. attempts to keep his commentary going)

But here at the sharp end, in the cold, muddy foothills of the Falkland Islands, with the rain pouring down and gunfire raining down on us, the very real and harsh nature of this all-too human conflict –

Studio manager: Sorry, Wallace. 'Avin a bit of trouble with the sounds. Could you run through that last bit again, mate? Start from 'But here at the sharp end . . . '

*

(Sound of tape going wonky, then stopping)

Wallace Arnold: I'm – I'm – I'm awfully sorry, a small 'hiccup' there of a most proverbial nature! Must have been a practice tape! That's technicians for you!

(Coughs. Final noise of farmyard animals)

Suffice to say that my *Arnold at War* series earned me the legendary Outstanding Achievement Award from the British Wireless and Steam Radio Association, presented in a live ceremony from the Guildhall by the then recently-elected Deputy Leader of the Labour Party, my old friend and quaffing partner, Mr Roy Hattersley:

*

(Applause)

Roy Hattersley: Ladies and – not to put too fine a point on it! – Gentlemen, as someone who himself occasionally keeps the bailiffs at bay by earning a paltry crust through employing his skills as a light essayist in the proud tradition of Chesterton and Jack Priestley – and let me add that, contrary to popular belief, I do not carry both volumes of the magisterial

Shorter Oxford Dictionary in my albeit capacious back pocket! – it affords me no small pleasure to raise whatever appendage may or may not be attached to my uppermost protuberance to a friend and fellow scrivener who, like me, shares a lifelong addiction to the Immortal Bard and who is also profoundly partial to the sound of leather on willow and the sport associated therewith. I give you the man who continues to welcome us to his most agreeable world, Ladies and Gentlemen, the Voice of British Broadcasting – Mr Wallace Arnold!

(Applause)

*

Wallace Arnold: Thus the new, positive tone for the Eighties was set. From the marriage of His Royal Highness the Prince of Wales to Lady Diana Spencer in 1982, through the appointment of my old friend Jeffrey Archer as deputy leader of the Conservative Party in 1986, to the abandonment of the old rates system in 1989, the Eighties stood for energy, optimism and the power of Positive Thinking. At long last, the moaning minnies were on the run, and a new spirit of get-up-and-go pervaded the country. This was the mood I tried to convey when I took over the stewardship of that doughty consumer programme *You and Yours* while Miss (Ms!) Patti Coldwell was on holiday in the Summer of '85:

*

Wallace Arnold: Hello. This is Wallace Arnold saying, 'Welcome to my Wireless, Welcome to my World', and Welcome to another edition of *You and Yours*.

(You and Yours *Theme Music*)

In recent months, there has been increasing concern voiced at home and abroad about the current safety standards on many household appliances. Just last week, we heard of the distressing case in Torquay of a young woman who placed her hand in a toaster for a full two minutes because the manufacturers had simply not made it clear that their appliance could in no circumstances double as an oven-glove. And yesterday from Hartlepool came the news of a 53-year-old man rushed to hospital with a suspected bone fracture after tying his shoelace too tight. Once again, the footwear manufacturers in question had failed to make it clear that if pulled too tight, the common shoe-lace can be a potential health-hazard. I have with me here Mr Kenneth Hornsworth from the Consumer Rights Society, 'Protect'.

Mr Hornsworth: Good afternoon.

Wallace Arnold: Mr Hornsworth, isn't it about time you and your wretched ilk stopped all this bleating at the taxpayer's expense every single day at 12 noon? Have you never heard of common sense? Good lord, pull yourself together, act like a man, stand on your own two feet and take your footling gripes elsewhere! Thank you for joining us, Mr Hornsworth.

Mr Hornsworth: I really must –

Wallace Arnold: And that leaves us with another, hmm, let me see, twenty-two and a half minutes of this edition of *You and Yours*. Time, I think, for a selection of some of my own – and I trust *your* own – best-loved tunes, including this one from that evergreen master of melody Mr Frank Sinatra:

(Frank Sinatra sings 'My Way'. Fade)

*

Wallace Arnold: The Eighties ended with a tremendous wave of freedom, dislodging the dictatorships of the Eastern Bloc; no wave more welcome than that which gave Nicolae and Elena Ceaucescu of Rumania a soaking. Coincidentally, I had visited this unsavoury couple only the previous year, as the guest presenter of *Down Your Way*. It was a brave programme, full of incisive criticism delivered under difficult conditions. I have no doubt that the tone of standoffishness and irony in my report reminds the listener that it takes a lot more than a Communist dictator to pull the wool over the Arnold eyes!

*

Wallace Arnold: And here I am inside the Presidential Palace, and jolly charming it is too. Nicolae, you've been President of this lovely country for how many years now?

Nicolae Ceaucescu: Twenty-four years.

Wallace Arnold: Twenty-four years! My goodness! Well, you're looking very well on it I must say, and so too is your wife, Elena. Now, Elena, this splendid Presidential Palace must take quite some effort to keep clean!

Elena Ceaucescu: Is right.

Wallace Arnold: *(laughs)* I bet it does! A woman's work, eh!? But when you manage to grab the odd moment to yourselves, how do you put your feet up? Any hobbies or pastimes, Nicolae?

Nicolae Ceaucescu: Barbecue.

Elena Ceaucescu: Barbecue.

Wallace Arnold: Good for you! And jolly tasty too, I've no doubt! And what record would you like us to play for you?

Nicolae Ceaucescu: Frank Sinatra.

Elena Ceaucescu: 'My Way'.

*

Wallace Arnold: Luckily, I escaped with just five nights in the Guest Suite at the Presidential Palace, but others every bit as brave as myself were not, of course, so lucky.

I have called the Eighties the Thatcher Decade, and that doughty lady did indeed make it her own, as I was explaining to Dr Anthony Clare on my celebrated performance *In the Psychiatrist's Chair* at the end of 1989:

*

Dr Anthony Clare: And would I be right in thinking that Mrs Thatcher has been a very major influence on you?

Wallace Arnold: Yes, indeed. She's the most . . . *(deep breath)* . . . she's really everything . . . *(small sob)* . . . remarkable lady . . .

Dr Anthony Clare: Would it be fair to describe her almost, perhaps, as a mother figure?

Wallace Arnold: Not only a mother figure. In March of this year, she . . . she . . . she became a grandmother *(sobs)*. Lovely little baby boy. Michael, son of . . . son of . . . Mark! *(breaks down uncontrollably)*

Dr Anthony Clare: Come on now, deep breath. That's better. Big blow *(Wallace Arnold blows nose)*. All better. There's a brave boy.

*

Wallace Arnold: And so the decade ended on an emotional note, and it is on that note that I should like to leave you today. Who knows what the dread Nineties still have in store for us? But of one thing you may be sure: through all the ups and downs, through bad times as well as good, my familiar voice will be here, with you in your drawing rooms, saying, as always, 'Welcome to my Wireless. Welcome to my World'.

The Thatcher Foundation

It is with no small measure of regret that I announce
the rejection by our once-proud nation of a very great
female who took us out of recession and into the land
of plenty. I speak, of course, of Margaret Thatcher,
who has been left to fend for herself in her South
London mock-Georgian style maisonette with hob,
downstairs 'toilet' (dread word!) and twin garage
facility.

As is well known, the name of Arnold, Wallace is the
prime adornment upon the freshly-minted writing paper
of the Thatcher Foundation, some way above Thatcher,
Mark and one down from Archer, Jeffrey. The aim of
the Foundation – to which, I might add, the sum of
£235.67 has already been donated from a variety of
sources, after a period of only two months – is to
promote the beliefs of Mrs Margaret Thatcher, while
at the same time providing that magnificent lady with
something to 'keep her busy' over the next decade or
so. Might I take this opportunity to beg all readers of
The Spectator, however hit by the present recession, to
contribute a little something to this great cause. It would
be sad indeed if this country were to allow this doughty
warrior to remain in her present state, alone and
unwanted, a mere shadow of her former self.

Without going into too great detail, I feel duty-bound
to paint a 'pen-portrait' of a visit I paid to the Dulwich
homestead only last week. I was there to deliver by
hand a major gift to the Thatcher Foundation. It was

an envelope from a variety of major city institutions who wished to show a token of their gratitude to this remarkable lady. It contained a Boots voucher worth £4.35, redeemable at over 600 stores throughout the country, plus attractive greetings card with verse. This, I felt sure, would do much to perk the lady up, and I looked forward to glimpsing the lustre as it returned once more to her eyes.

Envelope in hand, I pressed the bell of the Dulwich maisonette. Before the fifth chime had sounded, the door swung open. There stood a forlorn figure clad in viyella housecoat and fluffy slippers of floral design, one hand clasping the butt of a cigarette, the other clutching lamely at a jar of Windolene. Mis-aimed lipstick lent colour to her left cheek. 'Margaret!' I sighed, my voice faltering. A tear came to her eye. 'Wallace,' she answered, 'Is it really you?' I held out the envelope. 'Take it, Margaret, I implore you!' I exclaimed. 'The CBI have had a whip-round. They would be most awfully upset if you were to refuse!'

She nodded me indoors. Framed photographs of her sharing a laugh with President Trudeau and greeting President and Mrs Reagan in the VIP lounge at Heathrow lay hugger-mugger on the uncarpeted floors. The cobwebbed telephone lent a bleak resonance to a sitting room furnished only with a solitary beanbag. On the kitchen table stood a beaker replete with a lone straw and a double measure of Windolene.

'They still mention you in the Commons, you know,' I tried to reassure her. 'Well, not *you* exactly, but quite a few of your achievements – Poll Tax and so on. You've carved yourself a place in history.'

Margaret removed the Capstan from her mouth and sighed. 'Eeh bah gum,' she said, 'there's nowt so queer as folk.'

One has long prided oneself on one's ear for accents, and it did not take me long to divine that Margaret had shed years of elocution in order to revert to the lingo of her roots. At the same time, she placed a pan on the hob, poured in the dregs of a Mazola bottle, and set to work on creating a 'chip buttie' for herself.

As she walloped the bottom of the jar of Daddies Tomato Ketchup with a force that belied her femininity, I sought to deliver some heartening news in her direction. 'The Thatcher Foundation is making excellent progress, you'll be glad to hear,' I said. 'And with the funds so far accrued, we have high hopes of announcing a headquarters early next week.'

'Yer'll be buyin' summat grand, ah trust,' she said, her mouth half-full with chips and Mother's Pride, 'summat down t'Strand or in t'Mall?'

'A part share in a Scout hut near Epping two nights a week is more the ticket,' I replied. 'It's all our funds stretch to at the mo. But I'm sure things will pick up. We have a solid pledge from a major consortium of Midlands industrialists for £7.50, and there may well be more where that came from.'

But for the time being she seemed to have gone off into a world of her own, appearing to mistake something in the far corner of a frying pan for her old cabinet colleague Lord Young of Graffham. A tear entered her eye. 'Others bring me problems,' she said, her old, beautifully modulated voice returning, 'but you, David, you bring me solutions!'

'Margaret,' I said, gently clutching her arm. 'That is not Lord Young. It is a smear of cooking fat.' But she was far, far away, lost in happier times.

Things that Need to be Said

I GIVE THE PRINCE OF WALES A VOICE

An irresponsible slur was perpetrated last week on the Prince and Princess of Wales by this very newspaper. A delightfully ordinary photograph of a normal, happy family enjoying some fruit off a silver salver with their horse while sitting on wickerwork seats in the middle of a field was held up to ridicule in the most monstrous fashion. I trust the following *vignettes* serve as a useful antidote.

My own involvement with our future King goes back yonks. I remember well the morning a full fifteen years ago when I answered the incessant trill of the telephone (dread contraption!) to find myself summoned to Kensington Palace. Looking relaxed and cheerful in the full-dress uniform of the Commander in Chief of the 2nd King Edward VII's Own Gurkha Rifles, Prince Charles drew me to one side and informed me that he felt his public image was too crusty.

'But my spies tell me,' he confided, 'that you share my positively Goonish sense of humour!'

'Ying-tong-iddle-i-po!' I exclaimed.

Needless to say, we both fell about, and at that very moment he engaged me on an informal basis as his principal speechwriter. Having exchanged a few more immortal Goonish catchphrases ('needle, nardle, noo!'), we collected a horse and a couple of wickerwork chairs and repaired to a nearby field to discuss topical matters over a silver salver of artificial fruit.

I was to discover that, beneath those mellifluous jests,

there lay a very deep and thoughtful young man, with firm views about the future of the world. 'Houses,' he said to me that first afternoon. 'People live in houses, and that is as it should be.' I nodded my agreement. He continued. 'And a house without windows is like, is like, is like – why, it's like *a totally windowless house*. Houses simply *must* have windows.'

At this point, I looked up from my notebook. 'I think, sir,' I exclaimed, 'I can feel a speech taking shape.' Six months later, the Prince of Wales was to deliver his famous 'A Crying Need for Windows' speech to the Royal Institute of British Architects. 'The window,' he was to conclude, 'is, in a very real way, the only means by which a person within a house can see outside. This, I feel, we may be in grave danger of forgetting.' Within the profession, it caused a stir, but to the country at large his future role as the architectural conscience of the nation was now assured.

Soon there was no stopping him. Under the watchful eye of Arnold, he developed firm ideas concerning roads ('Frankly, there is little or no point in building a new road if it fails in its basic purpose of going from point A to point B'), agriculture ('It is all too easy to forget that crops will only grow if someone first takes the trouble to plant them'), wildlife ('It would behove us all to remember that in many important respects the giraffe differs from the human being') and conservation ('You know, I sometimes wonder how many things that we value would be with us today if our ancestors had not taken the trouble to conserve them'). Here, evidently, was a young man to whom people had to listen, and whose views on everything from the Arts ('a terrific boon') to food ('essential for man's survival') were gaining him increasing respect from the community at large.

Meanwhile, his sense of humour – incorporating, I might add, our shared taste for the disgraceful pun! – never faltered. 'I may be the Prince of Wales,' he quipped in an after-dinner speech to The Grand Masonic

Lodge of Royal Kircudbrightshire, 'but frankly I try not to "wail" – that's W-A-I-L – all the time!' On another occasion – in an address to the Young Farmers Association – he memorably quipped, 'In front of an audience such as this, there is, I fear, a need to make my choice of words somewhat "wheaty", or, to put it another way, "witty', but pronounced "wheaty"!'

As the Prince of Wales prepares for his next speech, this time on the car ('I sometimes feel we might be growing too dependent on the four-wheeled vehicle, useful item though it is'), those who run this newspaper should recall his words to the Townswomen's Guild of Northumbria back in 1988: 'To my mind, criticism is justified when – and only when – events serve to justify that criticism'. We would do well today to ponder the wisdom of those words.

TVam

I have long been known as one of this country's foremost campaigning journalists, but never more so than now. A grievous injustice has occurred, and it is up to those of us who continue, against the odds, to harness a deep sense of right and wrong to make our voices heard above the din.

I refer, of course, to this week's shabby and disgraceful treatment of TVam. It goes without saying that my previous campaigns have been hard hitting (I refer of course to my long-running espousal of the introduction of the collected works of Elizabeth David to the O and A level English Literature syllabus, my six-year quest to change the name of Hampstead's Mandela Mansions to the more agreeable Worsthorne Mews, and my long-term tussle with the BBC to pronounce the word 'off' not with an ugly short 'o', but in its original and correct mode as 'orf' or 'awf', to rhyme with cough – or 'cawf'), but I promise you this. I will not rest nor budge an inch until I see the return of Mike Morris, Ulrika the Weathergirl, the famous Sunday 'caption competition', Carol Thatcher and Roland Rat to our screens.

Deep breath, Wallace, deep breath. My connection with TVam goes back to its formation in 1983, when my own good self, Peter Jay and David Frost decided to offer the viewer the best news service in the world. Adapting this excellent policy to early hiccups, we soon found that we could offer the viewer a far more comprehensive news service by cutting bulletins to three and a half minutes on the hour, every hour, and introducing such well-loved favourites as Kartoon Kapers, Today's Pop Video, Rusty Says 'Ravioli Can Be Fun', 'Shape Up with Shirley', 'Your Magic TV Moments', 'Weep Awhile with Caring Clare' and our hard-hitting travel documentary series, 'With Kylie Down Under'.

By Spring, 1990, we had rescheduled our extensive worldwide news service to ninety seconds (including advertising break) in the much-coveted 6.35am slot, and we were delighted in October '91 to win general acclaim for our Gulf Coverage. This included on-the-spot studio reports from top TV presenter, Mike Morris, discussing weather in the war-zone with visiting celebrity Jason Donovan. There was also the hard-hitting 'Moggies for Our Boys' appeal, whereby viewers could send family pets direct to the Gulf for British troops to cuddle and fuss over and, of course, our momentous 'Profile of a Dictator' series, featuring an in-depth profile by leading experts of Johnny Sparkle, heart-throb lead singer of The Dictators rap group.

Much credit for the formation of this comprehensive news and current affairs service must go to Bruce Gyngell (correctly pronounced 'Jingle'), whom I had been responsible for hiring after the initial hiccups of our opening days. Bruce had previously worked as Deputy Governor of the prestigious Coonawarra Top-Security Facility for Hardened Offenders, with special responsibilities for corrective discipline, but he had become increasingly keen to branch out into the field of light entertainment.

Within days of his appointment, he had demonstrated a tremendous flair for the popular touch. The Jay/Frost regime had, he argued, been aiming too high, and one of his first acts was to remove both A. J. P. Taylor from his post as weatherman and Anita Brookner as presenter of 'In Town Tonight', to be replaced by, respectively, Ulrika the Weathergirl and an attractive glove puppet called Cuddles.

I must now pass on to the frankly upsetting area of the franchise scandal.

Bruce had often urged upon Margaret (Thatcher) a more monetarist approach to the great liberal dinosaur of British television. Consequently, Margaret decided upon a system that awarded each franchise to the highest bidder. In full consultation with myself, David Frost, and all other members of the board of directors, Bruce Gyngell decided to make an extremely well-judged bid of £14 million. Scandalously in my opinion, our closest competitors, Sunrise, bid £34 million *and yet they were awarded the franchise!* The full and bitter disgrace of this travesty will be immediately apparent to one and all. Finally, may I add that it is our loyal viewers for whom I feel sorriest. I can reveal that we had been planning a third showing of 'With Kylie Down Under' for the Spring of '93, and this they will now be denied through the high-handed decisions of the ITC. Yes, Margaret, I, too, am heartbroken, and so are many millions of others.

A view of the Gulf

NO PLACE FOR PERSONAL FEELINGS

Might I 'kick off' this column by thanking my many admiring readers for their congratulations on the occasion of my well-publicised engagement to Lady Panatella Slimm? Though her past has, indeed, been somewhat checkered – a brief engagement to Mr 'Doc' Cox of *That's Life*, followed by a short entanglement with Sir Harold Acton, came only a few months after a somewhat lengthier *liaison* with Mr Noddy Holder of the popular singing group Slade, which itself followed two well-intentioned but ultimately unsuccessful marriages: first to the young Mr (later Lord) St John Stevas and second, during an ill-advised 'hippy' phase, to Mr 'Teasy-Weasy' Raymond – she is now anxious to 'settle down' with a true gent who can offer her – what? – stability, *savoir faire*, a marvellous sense of humour, political acumen and, I trust, an agreeable set of table manners.

But to more serious matters. It is what one might term an 'open secret' that no less a being than W. Arnold esq. is the brains behind many of Fleet Street's most challenging and intellectually rigorous editorials. In these days of strife, rarely a morn hath passed without a call from one eager-beaver editor or another, anxious to inveigle me onto his editorial 'Gulf think-tank'. I reprint the following extracts from my personal *Gulf Diary* as an offering to those of my readers who wish to study how one civilised man comes to an informed opinion about matters so important, while never allowing his private life to intrude.

*

Jan 15th Lady Panatella awakes me with a frothy Cappucino. Have never known such happiness. Write *Daily Mail* leading article, 'This Talk of War is Bunkum: Let us Make Merry by Leading War Expert Wallace Arnold'.

Jan 16th I fail to notice her new earrings, so Lady Panatella wants to call the whole thing off. I tell her she is bossy. Row ensues. I write main feature for the *Daily Express*: 'Stamp Out this Odious Tyrant – Now'.

Jan 17th Last night, I offered a gentlemanly apology; Lady Panatella melted in my arms. Never such bliss! Today, I write main *Telegraph* think-piece, 'A Time to Lay Down Arms and Negotiate'.

Jan 18th Lady Panatella allows me to go 'all the way'. I pen a robust essay for *The Spectator*, under the heading, 'The Bombing of Baghdad: Let's Go All The Way'.

Jan 19th Lady Panatella sends out for new sheets. I continue the main thrust in a brilliantly-observed piece in *The Sunday Telegraph*, beginning, 'War is, in many respects, like sex. There is no reason why it should not be performed with joy and pride but, in the final analysis, a mopping-up operation is sadly inevitable'.

Jan 20th I treat Lady Panatella to a slap-up lunch. The bill is absurdly high, but I think I can 'lose it' on expenses. In the afternoon, I nip into the *Daily Mail* to pen a forthright leader, 'The True Cost of The Gulf Operation', arguing that we can charge it to our Allies. I argue that, in time of war, there is no place whatsoever for personal feelings.

Waiting for Madonna

SEX (DREAD WORD!)

My eyes positively lit up. The editor of the *Independent on Sunday* newspaper had asked me if I would write an essay about my dinner. My friends invariably accuse me of being the veritable *doyenne* of food writers so I found myself agreeing forthwith. It was only some minutes later that I discovered, with no little disappointment, that he wished me to write not about my dinner but *Madonna*.

It emerged that the *Independent on Sunday*, responsible, 'up-to-the-minute' (!) newspaper that it is, had spent a great deal of money in securing the rights to a small portion of the aforesaid Madonna's latest *oeuvre*, *Sex* (dread word!). For the full five thousand pounds, seventeen shillings and sixpence, we are now legally entitled to reproduce:

(a) three (3) buttocks, fully naked
(b) one (1) bosom, partially bared, and
(c) one head-shot of Sir Norman Fowler with spectacles.

(The last-named item being acquired as a tie-in with the publishers, who are also responsible for Sir Norman Fowler's forthcoming *A Vision of Britain*, thus accounting for the additional seventeen shillings and sixpence).

For an extra £3000, the newspaper was entitled to send a leading representative to New York, there to peruse the aforementioned tome in conditions of strictest privacy. The editor had lined up a short-list of intellectuals for the task, the first being the great Argentinian scrivener Jorge Luis Borges. Alas, it had emerged that not only was there, as yet, no braille edition of the book available, but also that poor Borges had died a full three years ago.

The third choice was Dame Iris Murdoch, but she was 'pipped at the post' by the second choice – yours truly. My commission was to write an accompanying text of two thousand or so words emphasising the deep seriousness of the project, showing how the publication of three buttocks and one half-bosom was indeed a worthwhile and thought-provoking exploration of the nature of contemporary celebrity.

I arrived at the New York headquarters of Madonna's publishers, to be ushered with a copy of the tome into a gentleman's lavatory and directed to the cubicle bearing my own name. As I passed along the row of cubicles I noted the full range of well-respected authors and thinkers whose illustrious names were posted on the adjoining doors.

In the first cubicle, grunting learnedly, sat Mr Norman Mailer, reporting for that once-doughty journal, *The New Yorker*. The next cubicle betrayed odd swishing sounds which I can only imagine emanated from the inhabitant, Mr Martin Amis, in his struggle to pull the top off his felt-tip. In the third cubicle, my old friend and quiffing partner Mr Andrew Neil could be heard getting in trim for his forthcoming in-depth interview with the 'lovely lady'. In the fourth cubicle sat Mr Melvyn Bragg, reciting over and over again in his sonorous Cumbrian voice a freshly-composed extract from his new book, in which the hero, Martin Bagg, a highly successful Northern television producer and Booker Prize-winning novelist, finds himself in bed with the world-famous pop-singer 'Gadonna', only to find himself questioning the very nature of his existence as he grapples with her suspender belt. Finally, there in the fifth cubicle was my dear mentor Lord Rees-Mogg, meticulously studying the work with high-powered binoculars in search of any stray sightings of artistically invalid flesh.

Taking my place in the sixth cubicle and carefully locking the door behind me, I opened the book with an intellectual excitement unequalled since my first reading of Proust. For the next hour, I studied those extraordinary photographs with a fierce intensity, breathlessly decoding the semiotics of celebrity, time and time again deconstructing the resonances of such polymorphous cultural weaponry, and urging myself on and on in my quest to ponder the palpable otherness of fame. I emerged from that cubicle breathless, yes, exhausted, yes, but also strangely elated. Next week, our magazine will proudly publish my definitive essay on the work, alongside full colour photos of the three buttocks and half a breast. Incidentally, reports on the recession, the cutbacks in the mining industry and news from abroad have now been re-scheduled for February, 1993.

Whither the Wireless?

THE LONG-LOST ART OF CONVERSATION

Whither the wireless? While the new Controller of the Third Programme (more like Out-Of-Controller, if you'll excuse the pun!) is hard at work reducing that once-noble station to a suitable dumping-ground for the unpleasing sounds of 'Wrap' and 'Reggie' music, the news comes winging its way that the Home Service is hell-bent on taking that most delightful of programmes, *Stop the Week* off the air.

I have, of course, been a mainstay of 'Stoppers', as we affectionately term it, for close on twenty-five years; indeed, with Mr Bob Robinson, Miss (Ms!) Ann Leslie, and Professor Laurie Taylor I was one of the original foursome, soon gaining a niche as the firm favourite of the great listening public for my unashamedly forthright opinions on such matters as pouring the milk in first when making a cup of tea ('unspeakable habit!'), the rights and wrongs of wearing a cravat ('splendidly, nay *delectably* English!') and the impossibility of a chap attempting 'that most unyielding of all household chores – namely the ironing!' Though I was undoubtedly the most popular member of the team, a team is what we were, the others all chipping in quite freely with their anecdotes and snappy comments, seemingly content in the knowledge that they would eventually be outshone by you-know-who!!

We were, in our humble ways, attempting to revive the long-lost art of conversation. Let others remain glued to the gogglebox. Bob, Ann, Laurie and Wallace were the standard-bearers for civilised chat of a type and quality unknown since the goodly Dr Johnson (though it had briefly been revived by our closest counterparts, the Algonquin Set, bless – as Uncle Bob might say! – their cotton socks).

The memories come flooding back. Classic moments abound. To pay due credit to my fellow panellists, the anthologists will undoubtedly wish to record the gorgeous waterfall of aphorisms coined at approximately 7.35pm on the night of Friday, September 30th, 1978. It all began when Bob asked the waspish Ann Leslie for her opinion on the vexed issue of piped music in restaurants. Quick as a flash, Ann replied, 'I am against pipes of all kinds in restaurants – and that includes piped music!' After much chortling and general delight from her fellow panellists, Ann said – with characteristic generosity – 'But I'm literally dying to know what *you* think, Bob!'

Never lost for a word, Bob replied, without so much as a second's hesitation, 'Well, Ann, you might be forgiven for failing to appreciate the finer points of piped *music* in restaurants, and I might even let you off the proverbial hook for – to coin a phrase! – turning your nose up at the type of pipe that one enjoys a jolly good puff on if one is of a smoking disposition but, by golly, I'll eat my hat if you tell me in all honesty that you are really against pipes *of all kinds* in restaurants – for have you not considered, perchance, how very chilly those estimable eating establishments would be were they not warmed in the winter months by the hot water *pipes* so admirably linked to their central heating systems?!'

Needless to say, we all fell about with laughter at such cleverness, but the hilarity did not end there. Within seconds, Professor Laurie Taylor had launched into his second best – possibly even his best – anecdote about central heating in restaurants, setting all of us rocking with mirth. The focus of attention then fell on yours truly. 'I can tolerate piped music,' I began. 'I can even feel duly appreciative of piped heating and I am, as you know, something of an inveterate pipe-smoker – indeed, I am the proud holder of the Pipesmoker of the Year Award, 1973 – but I stoutly refuse to give elbow-room to the *other* type of pipe, ha ha, – and that, may I add, is a promise!'

Alas, as the laughter subsided, the programme came to an end, the familiar jaunty beat of the title tune drowning out the subsequent chat, so that I cannot now, for the life of me, remember to what other type of pipe I was referring. Nevertheless, I hope this small gem of a chat will have inspired many readers to prac- tice the long-lost art of conversation in their own homes. Just a few minutes a day, and you too could be a match for the immortal Bob, Ann, and Laurie – or even my own good self!

Xmas at Windsor

OF WIZENED RAISINS, BLACKENED HANDS AND ROYAL FARTHINGS

Many readers of the daily and Sunday *Independent*, deprived by the newspapers' inverted snobbery of all knowledge of the comings and goings of our Royal Family, have specifically requested that I shed a little light on Christmas at Windsor in all its great pageantry and colour.

In the present day, the festivities commence after Chapel at 10.48 precisely when the Duke of Edinburgh recites from the formidable list of right royal puns he has managed to assemble over the course of the preceding year. 'I'm not musical, but I might just sit on DUKE Box Jury!' he exclaimed last year, and before the laughter had subsided he added, 'Let's hope my presence won't have THRONE them!'

At 10.58, the Queen herself takes to the rostrum. I believe it is not widely known that Lilibet's somewhat stern public image conceals a highly-developed sense of humour – with a weakness for the good old 'knock-knock' joke! Armed only with a small, neatly typed list, she begins, 'Knock Knock'. The rest of us chorus 'Who's there, ma'am?!' in gleeful expectation of a right royal rib-tickler. 'Queen Elizabeth II,' she responds. 'Queen Elizabeth II *who*?' we yell back in excitement. 'Just Queen Elizabeth II. The monarch need not employ a surname,' she replies. Guests may show their appreciation with a ripple of applause.

The Royal Family undertakes a great many ceremonies over this very special time of the year, many of them with the poor and needy in mind. House guests at Windsor are expected to assist with due solemnity at each of these ancient Christmas morning ceremonies:

The Royal Farthing

Each year at 11.17am on Christmas Day, the Official Windsor and Slough District Collector of Taxes is formally summoned to be handed a single farthing from the Royal Household. He must then recite the ancient words, 'That will not be necessary, ma'am,' before handing it back. Members of the family and Household guests are then expected to beat him over the head with rolled up copies of newspapers, shouting, 'Be off! Be off!', whereupon the District Collector of Taxes returns to his office for another year.

The Handing Over of the Shoes

Every fourth year, the local poor are required to foregather on a front lawn. They are then required to remove their shoes (if it is snowing, tradition dictates that they must also remove their socks). The Prince of Wales – assisted by guests and household staff – then collects all the various shoes into a large bag marked with the traditional *Fleur de Lys* and, amidst much cheering and flag-waving, sets fire to it. The poor then return home in their bare feet. This colourful pageant is intended to emphasise the unbridgeable gap between monarch and commoner, and is presided over by the Archbishop of Canterbury.

Come Christmas lunch at 12.54pm, the Queen will prove an exhilarating hostess. While the Duke of Edinburgh puts the finishing touches to some Great British Bangers on his beloved mobile indoor barbecue, The Queen will keep her guests and closely family on their toes by asking some wonderfully 'ice-breaking' questions! For instance, last year I heard that gracious lady ask her son HRH Prince Edward, 'Have you come far?' This made for a wonderfully relaxed atmosphere. Over luncheon itself, talk may revolve around any number of subjects, from the likelihood of a little sunshine later in the day to the undoubted benefits of an umbrella in wet weather. Luncheon is followed by a little light entertainment, traditionally provided by a much-loved showbiz duo. This year, Sir Peregrine Worsthorne and Lady Lucinda Lambton have kindly agreed to sing a selection of old Nina and Frederick standards.

After the performers have been awarded their traditional Wizened Raisin, the servants will be called in for the ancient pageant of:

The Blackening of the Hands

This dates from 1856, when Queen Victoria first realised that, if carried in the hand, coal can leave a film of disagreeable dark dust. Prior to this, that venerable lady had imagined coal to be made of a light spongey substance. To commemorate this Royal discovery, the servants of the table line up with their hands outstretched while members of the Royal Family good-naturedly blacken them with specially-provided lumps of coal, before being formally scolded and sent on their way to enjoy, as I hope my devoted readers will also enjoy, a Most Merry and Charming Christmas.